Pursuing Enterprise
Outcomes

ALEX YAKYMA

Pursuing Enterprise
Outcomes

Maximizing Business Value
and Improving Strategy for
Organizations and Teams

ISBN: 978-0-9981629-2-8 (print)
ISBN: 978-0-9981629-3-5 (ebook)

In memory of Ivan and Antonina Yakyma,
beloved grandparents
who survived the most devastating war,
and dedicated their lives
to bringing the light of education to thousands of people

Contents at a Glance

Detailed Contents

CHAPTER 1

The Killer of Organizational Performance

The Impact of Crucial Connections

What does this picture tell you?

Map 1-1

Would you be surprised to find out that it represents two professionals, connected to one another in some way? What could that connection be? Maybe they are two developers working on the same software feature or two marketing professionals creating a campaign together. Whatever the connection is, they interact with each other to produce value and that's what the picture indicates.

1

How about this one?

Map 1-2

Your brain has likely already registered that "there's something wrong with the connection" and maybe that "the interaction is broken".

Diagrams like Map 1-1 and Map 1-2 are a central visual tool used throughout this book and are called interaction maps. *Interaction maps* are straightforward, intuitive diagrams that allow you to capture, analyze, demonstrate, and communicate the landscape of interaction in your enterprise. The nodes on the map don't need to be people: interaction maps might show the interactions of different kinds of assets or even concepts that matter to organizational performance. And the links that connect the nodes don't have to indicate collaboration but can encompass a wide variety of connections vital to a complex task. Later in the book, we will consider, for example, how assets—such as a software product—are connected to business outcomes. Those connections also constitute an interaction map.

Real-life interaction maps are more complex than the two-node example above and include more nodes, more connectors, and additional parameters. The ultimate goal of using interaction maps is to identify high-impact areas of improvement for an organization or a team.

In complex tasks that involve multiple people, interaction is a key enabler of high performance. A very typical example provides a good illustration:

Brenda and Jayden are software developers working on a new feature for their company's cargo tracking system. Both of them are fully dedicated to this task, and both are located in the same office building. They have worked together before, know each other well, and there's no significant impediment preventing them from effectively interacting on a daily basis. In this case, we would apply a map identical to Map 1-1:

Brenda

Jayden

Map 1-3

Under these conditions, they are able to work productively on the feature, and they soon deliver a good result.

Now, let's modify some of the parameters. If Jayden is many time zones away, he can no longer interact with Brenda as before. This single change in circumstance prevents them from working together as effectively as they used to. It is harder for Brenda and Jayden to find overlap time, to have screen-sharing sessions or video calls where they could "take a quick look at this code" or "quickly model something out on the virtual whiteboard". Little by little, Brenda and Jayden accumulate disconnects. They spend more time debugging divergences in their code, and less time actually advancing new functionality. When asked about the effect of limited overlap time, they agree that the disconnects have slowed them down by about 25%.

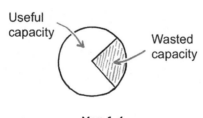

Useful capacity

Wasted capacity

Map 1-4

Now we've identified a disconnect, let's show it on our inter-action map:

Map 1-5

If we now say that Brenda and Jayden also have different pro-fessional backgrounds and different skill-sets, a new disconnect appears: they actually speak different "languages". This disconnect creates more recycles in their work and those recycles are hard to spot. Brenda and Jayden think they understand each other, but they interpret the same task differently, causing themselves more work later.

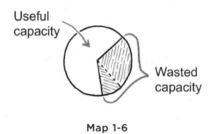

Map 1-6

Our interaction diagram now shows two degrees of separation:

Map 1-7

It often proves useful to label the disconnects for future reference. (We could keep track of the disconnects without labels in this simple two-person case, but in a large and more complex map, clarity is everything.)

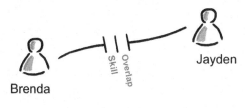

Map 1-8

Continuing our example, imagine that Brenda and Jayden have developed a personal disagreement: Jayden said some horrible things about Brenda's approach to non-serializable objects, and in response, Brenda suggested that she would have preferred feedback from someone who actually understands what non-serializable objects are used for in the first place. As a result, the amount of rework increases as Brenda and Jayden avoid virtually all interaction, unless absolutely necessary. Our map and performance levels have changed:

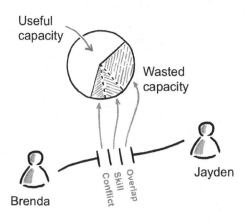

Map 1-9

The useful capacity appears to be a lot lower than one would expect.

Disconnects in a System

But the disconnect between Brenda and Jayden is not unique. Brenda and Jayden also have various disconnects with an internal customer. Some of those complications arise because both Brenda and Jayden are very technical types, and are not very proficient in the language of the business. Many of the technical folks in the organization don't even see this as a problem. Additional disconnects exist because Brenda and Jayden don't actually talk to the customer directly. There are two other employees separating them from the customer: a so-called product owner (PO), and the business venture coordinator (BVC).

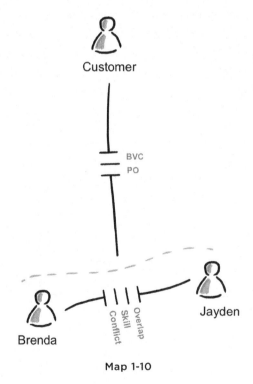

Map 1-10

Effective communication under these conditions is a challenge. The customer pressures the business venture coordinator to get new features completed as fast as possible. The BVC then goes to the PO, who considers that "no" is not an acceptable answer, regardless of the technical challenges or even capacity shortage. As a result, the team is always overloaded and produces low-quality solutions requiring rework, and ultimately taking up additional capacity.

But even this is not the full picture: we need to take a look at the role of the customer. Our customer is actually just a requester of work, a person who defines the requirements. The end users are a different set of people, who will actually consume that work. They are not consulted at all in this process, because the requester is confident enough in her own business expertise, and because the consumers have day jobs and don't like being interrupted with requests for input.

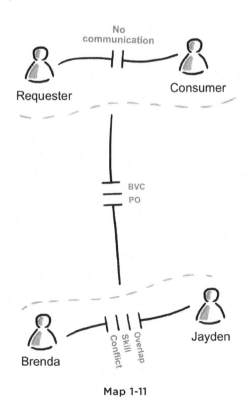

Map 1-11

The consumers struggle to adopt the solution that is delivered to them through this process. The requester, realizing that something has gone terribly wrong, requests a long laundry list of changes she believes will solve the problem. As a result of the complications, she and the business venture coordinator have to ask their big boss for more money because the project budget has been depleted. Where did the money go? It slipped away through organizational disconnects, leaving behind limited useful capacity for the team to translate into real customer value:

Map 1-12

This picture may shock a manager who is operating under the premise that their global workforce strategy and customer interaction are working fine, with perhaps some minor inefficiencies. But this manager has not paid attention to either the actual value delivered or the real cost involved.

The major types of disconnects on our map are: 1) disconnects among developers, 2) disconnects between developers and the customer, and 3) disconnects within the customer domain (between the requester and the consumer). Most of these disconnects tend to reinforce one another.

To show how disconnects reinforce one another, let's simplify the interaction map, leaving only substantial disconnects of types 2 and 3:

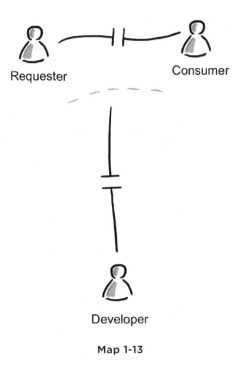

Map 1-13

In this scenario, the requester assumes they fully understand what the consumer needs, and only gets in touch with the consumer when work is being released to them. The requester and developer speak different "languages": the requester doesn't understand technical mumbo-jumbo, while the developer filters out the business jargon. They agree with each other because neither one is capable of spotting an inconsistency in the other's words. Here's how their interaction progresses over time, step by step.

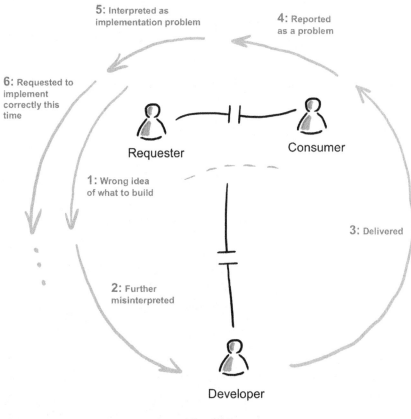

5: Interpreted as implementation problem

4: Reported as a problem

6: Requested to implement correctly this time

Requester

Consumer

1: Wrong idea of what to build

3: Delivered

2: Further misinterpreted

Developer

Map 1-14

Step 1: The request for new functionality comes from the requester. The requester is unaware of the disconnect with the consumer.

Step 2: The developer misinterprets the request and builds something different to what the requester originally intended.

Step 3: The developer releases new functionality to the consumer. The consumer is surprised, unable to make sense of the solution.

Step 4: The consumer reports to the requester that the solution is unsuitable and fails to satisfy their needs.

Step 5: The requester carefully analyzes the solution and realizes it has not been implemented as requested. The requester is unaware that the problem originates *in the requirements themselves*, and assumes the solution has been rejected by the consumer because the developer didn't implement the requirements properly.

Step 6: The team goes back and updates the solution to match the initially posted requirements, initiating a whole new sequence.

And the cycle repeats.

The numerous disconnects add up to a substantial amount of waste, typically invisible to the organization. One of our objectives is to bring clarity to this problem and help devise a path to recover proper connections:

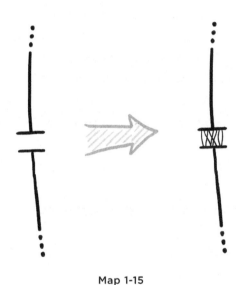

Map 1-15

In the next chapters, we will look at the causes of disconnects, and various strategies we can use to address and resolve them.

This and other chapters contain "Taking Action" section that provides suggested steps you can take to improve performance in your organization or team. The only type of knowledge that matters is the one that translates into action!

⁙ Taking Action

1 Identify the connections that determine the success of your work (it can be a project or other form of initiative):

   a Which of these have disconnects?

   b How do the disconnects impact your group's productivity?

2 Express your findings as an interaction map, using labels to add more context if needed. If the map grows overly complex it may end up being unreadable: "zoom out" and leave only the most impactful connections in the system.

3 Make a meaningful voice-over for that map. Your map should be a supporting structure for the story you are trying to express.

4 Use your interaction map to communicate the problem to other people in your group.

   a Present your map with a good storyline your audience can relate to.

   b Be open to suggestions and modifications. Adjusting an existing diagram leads to deeper understanding, and shares the sense of ownership, making it "their map" rather than just yours.

   c Strive for a "shared view" most of the participants can agree with. "Agreeing on the problem" is a strong prerequisite to successful problem resolution.

5 Run a quick problem-solving session. Aim at repairing one or two disconnects that matter the most, and plan for a first step in resolving them.

6 Establish follow-ups.

CHAPTER 2

How to Uncover Disconnects?

What Signals Do We Read?

While learning about disconnects and the impact they can have on an organization's productivity, we made an implicit assumption that we had full visibility of these disconnects. Generally speaking, this is not the case. There are important reasons why the visibility of disconnects is so low. To illustrate, we will look back at one of our previous examples.

Brenda and Jayden are in different locations, in time zones many hours apart. When there is no need for collaboration, geographical separation does not cause trouble. But Brenda, who is working with Jayden on a shared software feature, finds it much harder to establish productive collaboration with Jayden when compared with her local teammates in Austin. Brenda sees a causal connection between geographical separation and decreased progress on the shared feature. George is one of Brenda's bosses, a couple of levels above her. George is the one who actually made the strategic decision to move to a new and cheaper location, but he remains unaware of the consequences of his decision.

George is responsible for managing costs for Brenda's unit. He believes that if a person is assigned a task they are qualified to perform, that person will be a productive worker regardless of where they are located geographically. This belief, coupled with the constant cost-cutting pressure within the organization, informed George's decision to move some of the work to a lower-cost location. The natural assumption is that George would quickly learn his plan had created certain challenges, and some corrective action would be taken. But the levels of organizational hierarchy between Brenda and George act as an absorption layer, letting only good news through, and blocking anything that might disappoint the boss.

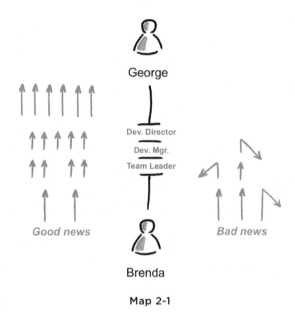

Map 2-1

The picture in George's mind is very far from reality. The organization underneath him acts as a pair of rose-colored glasses determining what George can and cannot see.

Map 2-2

Do things operate in this way because George has occasionally punished a bearer of bad news, teaching the layers of the hierarchy below him that bringing up problems is a really bad idea? This happens in some corporate environments but hasn't happened here. George is a very nice person and never punishes anyone for anything. A much subtler thing has developed instead, which leads to the same effect. Like most people, George genuinely likes good news, and at some point promoted a person who specialized in selective news delivery. The knowledge that the boss likes good news cascaded through all levels. Anyone who really cares about their career pays attention to this fact, and the system skews to selective filtering, as Map 2-1 demonstrates. As a result, George's beliefs are routinely validated, no matter how removed from reality they might be.

The systemic disconnect due to geographical separation remains unnoticed because of the systemic disconnect across the levels of the organizational hierarchy. This is a typical problem in many organizations that we can summarize as follows:

Systemic disconnects in an organization prevent the organization from seeing systemic disconnects.

Our task now splits into:

1   Understanding the disconnects in the system

2   Addressing the disconnects in a productive way

We will focus on the first part of the task in this chapter, and get to the second part of the task in later chapters.

How do we discover disconnects and the overall structure of interactions? There are a number of ways, but we will focus on the following:

1   Observation

2   Conversation

We will keep it that simple. It is best to keep your discovery system simple and to retain an open-ended approach so you increase your chances of catching important signals.

Observation

The first approach can be split into two subdomains: observation through indicators and raw observation.

Observation Through Indicators

As an example, let's assume an organization has a tool where the lifecycle of work items is being carefully maintained. The tool shows a simple timeline, with work items spread across multiple quarters:

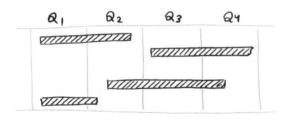

Map 2-3

Talking to various team members, leaders, and other subject matter experts reveals some interesting facts. For instance, the work items do not require as much effort as the timeline suggests, perhaps because quite a bit of waiting is involved. Poorly managed, emergent dependencies are the root cause of the problem:

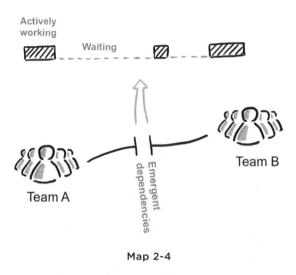

Map 2-4

Team A starts their work item but they have a dependency on team B. Team B already has other work, so team A must wait for team B to be able to take on their part of the task. This delays the value to the business. More importantly, it reduces the useful capacity of the teams. In fact, when a complex task is interrupted for a significant amount of time, the important tacit knowledge about the task dissipates *before* the group can leverage it. Implied knowledge will have to be recovered, and this takes additional effort. It can never be recovered perfectly, leading to errors and additional recycles:

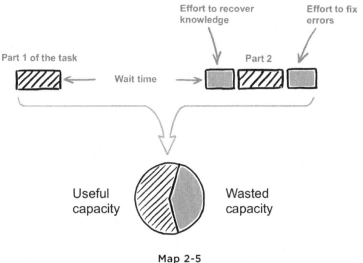

Map 2-5

This is one possible, common, scenario. But there can be others. You may discover, for example, that all tasks are pretty balanced in terms of duration and size. Does this mean there's no systemic delay? Possibly, but not necessarily. Teams can sometimes split a larger work item around dependencies, making their overall execution look good. But the real problem is obscured and the indicator is gamed.

These two duration-size balance scenarios demonstrate something important about complex environments:

There is no universally applicable set of indicators for diagnosing problems with complex tasks. To have an effective discovery process, indicators applicable to a particular task must be found.

This doesn't mean that generic metrics should not be collected, but that a metric, like task duration over size, may or may not reveal the problem.

Things can be even more complicated. Task durations displayed on the timeline may look very good:

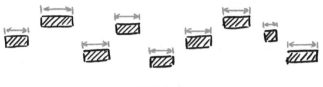

Map 2-6

This team doesn't split tasks around dependencies to make their task durations look better. This time the problem is elsewhere. Some of the items on the team's backlog are adjustments and fixes to previous work items that didn't function as well as intended. This delayed rework means that basic measures are no longer effective for discovering disconnects. Instead, rework must be linked back to the work item that caused it. When the *real* duration is calculated, and the proper items are connected with each other, the time view no longer looks as pretty:

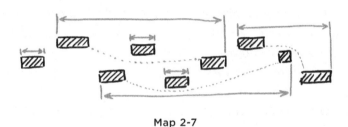

Map 2-7

To calculate the real duration we must distinguish between items that are independent and items that are rework from an earlier effort. Further investigation may reveal that the delayed rework is a result of poor interaction with the customer, and that's the disconnect we've been looking for:

19

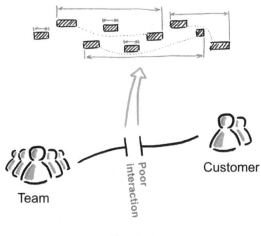

Map 2-8

Looking at task durations alone suggests that all tasks are executed in a fast and productive manner, and the disconnect is not visible. But when seemingly independent items are linked into a single whole, we can see the real durations are a lot less attractive. We can see where the true problem lies.

An important note: task lifecycle tracking usually focuses on tangible, quantitative measures and often completely ignores qualitative, intangible aspects of complex tasks, even though they are vital. We will discuss intangible outcomes in future chapters. Here we will only point out that the goal of every organization is more about delivering *value* than being *efficient* with their complex tasks. Important aspects such as customer satisfaction, usability, or safety, often end up being missing variables because they are intangible, and harder to capture and manage in a tool.

What if tasks are not being tracked at all? Even when they are, the organization may entirely misinterpret the data. Those not tracking task information might actually be better off in comparison to those who do track but fail to see a serious problem, misunderstand complex behavior, or even intentionally game the system. A huge number of organizations and teams take pride in flow efficiency when that flow delivers garbage. We must keep in mind that:

Increased focus on generic metrics, coupled with shallow interpretation of data, tends to reinforce disconnects rather than reveal them.

Raw Observation

Observing people in action has the potential to provide some missing answers. An old trick, used by many smart leaders, is to expose yourself to the actual task execution environment, rather than relying too much on metrics and status reports. This is a unique opportunity to discover potential disconnects and the overall nature of interaction.

The manner of observation matters a great deal. If done right, it may shed light on a lot of important things. If done poorly it might not uncover anything. Here are some useful tips for effectively leveraging raw observations:

1 Complex tasks often rely on intellectual effort more than physical work, so important aspects might be intangible and not directly observable in the physical environment. Therefore, disconnects are not usually between physical components on the production floor, but rather between the mental models of two professionals working on a common complex task. This type of disconnect requires deliberate exploration to be uncovered.

2 Expose yourself to the decision-making process of the people who work on the task. Much can be uncovered this way. Some of the typical activities are planning, various forms of work approval, prioritization events, funding discussions, and change management meetings.

3 Plug yourself into the process of routine status assessment and demonstration of the results. Note whether there is consistency between these observations and observations related to decision-making mentioned in 2.

4 Take notes; don't abbreviate. Contextual details vanish quickly and easily, leaving us with rapidly fading, shallow memories of things that actually mattered. Good, clear notes may help tell an important story when comparing various observations.

The next example is a team with a well-established, routine process of acquiring customer feedback on their new work "by demonstrating the current state of the system". The first flaw with the process is that the "customer" is not really a customer at all, but a customer representative who won't be using the system, so the usefulness of their feedback is questionable. Secondly, rather than demonstrating anything, the team merely reviewed the current tasks in the task list and updated the customer representative on the status, only mentioning current issues. This raw observation uncovers a significant disconnect in the environment:

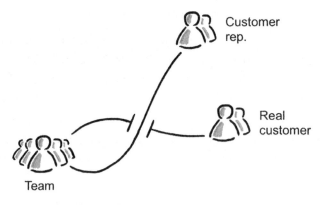

Map 2-9

The interaction map shows a well-established connection between the team and the customer representative causing a disconnect with the *real customer*. This is a pretty common situation that happens when the quality of feedback is poor because it comes from someone who has limited or no exposure to the actual usage context. This type of shallow feedback creates a false sense of understanding and blocks more meaningful forms of feedback.

One connection hijacks the other, and the actions taken as a result can be extremely costly and wasteful.

Conversation

Conversation is a powerful tool for progressive discovery and should be used whenever possible. A conversation may be completely unstructured, but it will be more helpful to have some rough structure prepared in advance, to provide a road map of the planned conversation, perhaps in the form of questions. On the other hand, too much structure may constrain the flow of conversation, so finding a balance is key:

With too little structure the conversation may not touch on some of the more important dimensions. With too much structure, the conversation cannot go beyond the script, which will prevent important facts from being uncovered.

Here are some additional tips:

1   Think of conversations as a process of exploring different hypotheses and validating them. Don't focus on just one possible explanation. Keep multiple hypotheses in mind until things become clearer. Be disciplined about questioning your current ideas, and do not underestimate your own confirmation bias! (Bringing in another person to team up with you in this endeavor can mitigate the influence of bias.)

2   Keep conversations short (under 30 minutes, for example), with a prepared set of seeding questions. Take notes during, or soon after, the conversation, paying particular attention to the *detail* of the other person's input, as this will be of most value later.

3   Keep conversations exploratory and open-ended. Don't ask questions that cut off effective discovery or reinforce confirmation bias. *Expect* to learn something new. If you only find support for your existing ideas, you are probably stuck in your discovery process. Take stock of your implicit assumptions and

see what kind of topics or questions might invalidate these assumptions, and offer a chance to get unstuck.

4   Ask the other person to provide examples to help you disambiguate their answers. Keep peeling the onion until you get to the core of a problem. Ask clarifying questions rather than relying on your own interpretation of their input. Leverage the tremendous opportunity this interaction format can give you, in a real-time progressive discovery.

5   Involve people in certain roles who might be able to provide a missing part of the answer. Cross boundaries boldly! The worst thing that can happen is that you learn more about the problem.

6   Protect the anonymity of people you have conversations with. Do not put people's names in your notes and avoid mentioning them verbally. In some corporate cultures, honest opinions lead to undesired consequences. Do not put good people in danger or be complacent in your own assessment of such danger.

7   Read your notes over and revise your hypotheses to determine whether you have enough evidence to validate or invalidate them. The same conversation might be interpreted differently as more knowledge about the problem is acquired.

In this example, Mary is exploring a problem and talking to Andrew about his team:

Mary: "How would you describe the level of collaboration in your team?"

Andrew: "We collaborate a lot!"

Mary: "What does 'a lot' mean?"

Andrew: "We basically collaborate on all work items, as a team ..."

Some people would accept that the team manifests a perfect example of collaboration, and would let the conversation end here, but Mary has more questions.

Mary: "So, what does this mean in terms of *specific* work items your team deals with? Who takes ownership over a work item, and how?"

Andrew: "One owner is assigned to each work item during planning."

Mary suddenly smells blood in the water.

Mary: "And then the collaborator just works with the owner on that task?"

Andrew (pausing for a second): "Not exactly … Everybody just owns the task they work on …"

Mary: "So, you said the team is collaborating a lot … and at the same time, it seems like everybody is contained within the scope of their own item. Where does their collaboration occur? Over what?"

Andrew: "Well, if someone occasionally gets stuck with their own item, they walk over to their teammate and have a quick discussion about it, ask a question, and so on."

Mary: "How often does this happen?"

Andrew: "Hmm … five to seven times a week … maybe …"

Mary: "Per person or per team?"

Andrew: "Per team."

Mary: "Would you say that is the total collaboration in your team environment?"

Andrew: "Well, no … These work items are often part of a higher-level item. We split a bigger item among team members, and work to deliver the pieces, which subsequently come together to a larger chunk of value."

Mary: "So, do the owners of smaller items touch base with each other every once in a while to see if the pieces are matching up?"

Andrew: "They do it once they are finished with their part, yes …"

Mary: "But not before?"

Andrew: "I guess not … no, not really …"

Mary: "How often does the process of putting those pieces together go smoothly?"

Andrew (smiling): "Not all that often …"

Mary: "What does the process usually involve?"

Andrew (now very serious): "Trying to make it fit together."

Mary: "And how long does it take … can you give me a rough idea?"

Andrew (staring at the ceiling for a bit): "It depends. It can sometimes add 20 percent, maybe even 50 percent, to the overall duration of the task."

Mary: "Do you think this could be alleviated by an earlier engagement of different task owners?"

Andrew: "I ... think so ... yes ... I guess we may not be as collaborative as we thought after all."

Mary: "Why is it the way it is, in your opinion?"

Andrew: "People are more comfortable with things this way, I suppose ..."

Mary: "Why do you think they'd be less comfortable establishing tighter collaboration? What would happen if two or more people owned a task, instead of one?"

Andrew (shaking his head): "They don't have the skills to do that."

Mary: "Please explain ..."

Andrew: "You see, we split larger tasks into smaller ones along skill lines to fit each team member's area of expertise ... They own a work item where they can add the most value."

Mary: "And how do those areas overlap with each other?"

Andrew (looking at Mary as if she had insulted him): "They don't."

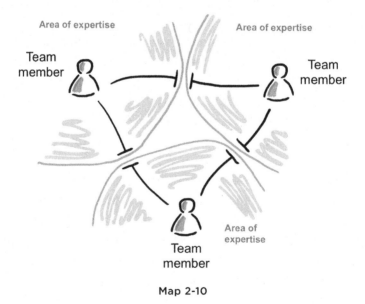

Map 2-10

Notice how different the ultimate takeaway is from the initial answer Andrew gave. Mary disambiguated Andrew's notion of collaboration, discovered the problem with collaboration on their team *and* a potential root cause. Mary's next step will likely be validating the hypothesis that team members struggle with their narrow specialization.

Mixing the Tools

Every tool has pros and cons, but using them together may help balance the cons of one tool with the pros of another. An important reason why raw observations are so useful an exploration method is that humans have a peculiar way of operating: our mental models do not translate into action exactly. This well-known process is called the "value-action gap". The gap is a result of an unconscious mental process: a person may genuinely believe one thing about their behavior and yet act completely differently when exhibiting that behavior. Such gaps are impossible to spot as a result of conversation only but can be helped if observation is added to the menu. On the other hand, observations also have limitations, and can only uncover actions but not necessarily the intentions. Relying solely on either conversation or observation might leave valuable information undiscovered. Let's look at another example:

Mary, as a result of a number of in-depth conversations, gained a solid impression from the teams about their approach to dealing with the unknowns that routinely occur during the execution of complex initiatives. Then, purely out of curiosity, she attended a regular planning session of one of the teams. One of the work items discussed was rewriting a module with complex formulas from a legacy technology platform into a new programming language. The group quickly decided that they would rewrite the module and then plug it into the system so that testers (who happen to be corporate users) could go over all the functionality to ensure it was working precisely as before, and prove the rewrite had been done correctly. Mary stuck to her mandate of being just an observer, but made a point of catching their leader Kayla after the session:

Mary: "Kayla, I think there's a big danger in applying the strategy you guys have selected for the task."

Kayla: "How come?"

Mary: "You may end up running into a lot of problems that could be prevented by proper testing."

Kayla: "But we intend to perform testing."

Mary: "Yes, at the very end, with end users, I know. That's precisely what worries me."

Mary explained to Kayla that there are plenty of potential problems with the formulas, with input and output formats, and so on. A small, consistent subset of the module's functionality should be validated early on, before rewriting the entire module. Validating this way might inform the way the rest of the rewrite was going to go.

Kayla: "I don't know if I follow what you're trying to say. I think we should involve Jeff. He's the developer who came up with the existing approach." She pulled out her phone and in a few minutes Jeff joined them and provided his peculiar rationale for the selected approach.

Jeff: "We can't carve out a small piece of that big task."

Mary: "Why not?"

Jeff: "Because, honestly, we don't know what the formulas in the code do. But if we rewrite it all, we don't actually have to worry what the calculations in the formulas stand for. We just translate the formulas from one programming language to the other and hope that it all works as before. If, on the other hand, we pick one formula, it's impossible to say what actual application-level process it participates in and what other formulas get involved, and whether we have to mock some additional data on the inputs, and so forth ..."

Kayla (now catching up with the problem): "So, we basically perform a blind rewrite?"

Jeff: "There's no need to be so dramatic ... But, well ... Yes."

The disconnect Mary helped to discover is a lack of expertise among developers, which leads to outrageous assumptions with poor validation strategy. It was Mary's balanced use of conversation and observation which uncovered the problem.

The Magic of Asking the Same Question

A simple but powerful tool for discovering disconnects lies in asking the same question to different people. When asked about the level of empowerment, for example, a team member might suggest a lack, while their manager suggests they thoroughly empower the team members. A discrepancy like this reveals a serious disconnect.

There is no exact science behind selecting the questions or respondents for inquiries like this, but here are some suggested groups of respondents which might help uncover disconnects:

- Managers vs. their subordinates
- Customers vs. producers
- Requesters/sponsors of work vs. consumers of work
- Representatives from different areas of expertise involved in the same product or providing the same service

This simple method is so powerful because it mitigates subjectivity by embracing divergences in opinions. A manager with a responsibility to empower teams may be biased to believe that they've succeeded, but the team doesn't have this bias. Team members may have an inclination to believe the opposite. While the team may be biased in assessing the results of their own efforts, asking the same question to the customer may provide the missing angle.

This method shouldn't be perceived as some sort of overly simplistic discovery mechanism. A closed-ended question like "How would you rate the team's ability to deliver quality service on the scale of 1 through 5?" could be asked of two different parties and a disconnect spotted as a difference in scores, but there will be much more value in open-ended questions. The same question could be asked as "How would you describe the team's ability to deliver quality service?", asking for a detailed account rather than a number. Comparing the detailed answers of the team to those of the customers will offer much more specific information, suggesting where the two parties are misaligned. The customer may appreciate the speed of delivery by the team but have an ongoing difficulty figuring out how to use delivered assets going forward, while the team does not provide sufficient guidance for that.

These are basic methods to use in your discovery process, and other tools will certainly provide additional leverage. Complex environments require relentless, open-minded exploration to uncover problems. Making problems visible is the first step to solving them.

👥 Taking Action

1   Pick an area of activity and apply observation techniques described in this chapter (observation through indicators and raw observation) to discover/explore disconnects.

2   For the same area, plan for some conversations with other participants of the process. These can range anywhere from more formal structured interviews to unstructured, casual chats. Compare, and see what works best for you.

3   Summarize findings across all observations. It is important to aggregate results into a brief set of meaningful takeaways. Make them presentable to others, and actually present them. Display leadership by driving the organization or team you are a part of towards resolving disconnects and improving the performance of your group.

CHAPTER 3

In Pursuit of Outcomes

Introducing Outcomes

When a manager is asked what one thing they would like to obtain, the answer is resoundingly, "More people!" It seems logical that more people will achieve more work, and this idea creates an undeniable feeling of potential, like an army on the march with nothing to stop them. Victory is never in doubt, because how can the focused strength of so many not translate into something absolutely glorious?

Very easily. Here are some examples of initiatives that despite a huge effort, did not deliver the results:

1   An HR team launches a new initiative to increase the motivation of the workforce and reduce attrition. After many months of hard work, they finally deliver an extended "employee package" including lots of perks, like company-sponsored gym memberships, meals, and better healthcare insurance coverage. When rolled out, this "solution" makes many people frustrated because the real problem is the huge differences in career opportunities between this organization and other similar organizations.

The mismatch only solidifies the employees' conviction that true career progression can only happen in other organizations, increasing attrition rather than reducing it.

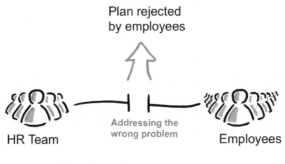

Map 3-1

The HR team gears up to deliver another iteration of the "solution" without understanding the real problem, repeating the mistakes of the first attempt.

2 A large organization launches a quality improvement initiative called "Black Diamond". A dozen experts with different backgrounds champion the initiative in their respective domains. Countless "Black Diamond" motivational posters are spread throughout the office, demonstrating the anticipated benefits and showcasing the proud champions. Two years into redefining processes and practices, the new, "quality-aware" way of operating has not materialized. The teams have continued to operate in the old way, but the leaders, reinforced by middle management, maintain a firm belief that "Black Diamond" was a success.

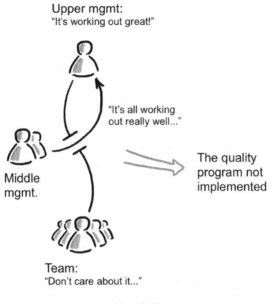

Map 3-2

Middle management pays lip service to upper management but doesn't mention the initiative to the teams anymore, to preserve any credibility.

3   A data analytics team creates a solution for their internal customer, replacing existing, very basic analytics capabilities with something more advanced. A month after being deployed, the new system is ditched by the customer, who turned out to prefer the original system. As a matter of fact, they never requested a new system but were happy to receive the advanced solution offered by the analytics team, especially if it comes at no expense of their own. They agreed to switch to the new system once it was delivered. But the new analytics system supplied nonsensical usage data. The customer didn't know the new system very well, and the analytics team lacked the domain knowledge to make sense of the analytics data. And the last thing the customer wanted was to spend any time troubleshooting the system they did not request in the first place.

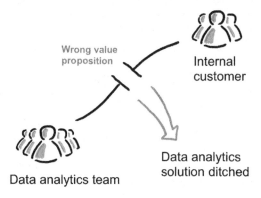

Map 3-3

A significant effort was wasted as a result.

4 An organization sends scores of middle managers to a leader-ship training course delivered by an external provider. Managers are trained in new behaviors, new ways of thinking, and new techniques, which is intended to help them increase perfor-mance levels in their teams. Unfortunately, none of what they've learned is applicable to their work environment. All attempts by individual managers to operate in a new way are blocked by the inertia of the organization's culture and incentive system. A lot of money was spent and nothing has changed. This was the sixth initiative of its kind, all with the same result.

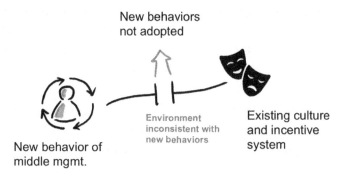

Map 3-4

5 An IT infrastructure project is intended to create a number of specific benefits, including increased revenues and a reduction of service costs, within a timeframe of two years. The initiative receives the desired approval due to its sound value proposition but does not deliver the intended benefits. Even so, the organization claims victory, suggesting that a great job has been done. In the meantime, the initial 2-year expectation is replaced with a 5-year timeframe.

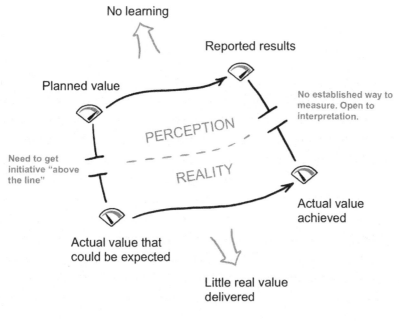

No learning

Reported results

Planned value

No established way to measure. Open to interpretation.

PERCEPTION

REALITY

Need to get initiative "above the line"

Actual value achieved

Actual value that could be expected

Little real value delivered

Map 3-5

All of these examples prompt the following observation:

In complex tasks, effort—no matter how hard—does not inevitably translate into a favorable outcome. A lot of hard effort may result in complete or partial waste, often unrecoverable.

The people in the examples above are genuinely willing to succeed with the task, and many of them are highly educated professionals with in-depth expertise. The problem in these situations is not the lack of expertise, or poor education, or even the lack of people, but the lack of clear understanding about what outcomes the effort is supposed to bring about. In other words, there's a fundamental disconnect between these two elements:

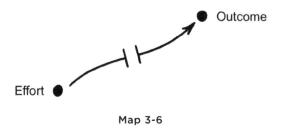

Map 3-6

How can organizations fail to notice such a seemingly obvious disconnect? Shouldn't the lack of a useful result be apparent to someone in the organization? Shouldn't something be done about it? Shouldn't everyone try to solve the problem? As it turns out, this type of disconnect isn't obvious at all. It remains obscure because all the attention that could go towards outcomes is hijacked by the organization's obsession with *outputs*. Outputs are a lot more tangible than outcomes, and so cause a short circuit in organizational cognition. Outputs are easier to think about, plan for, achieve, and measure, than the outcomes of work. An HR policy, for example, is a real, tangible deliverable. So is a quality process guardrail, an analytics software system, a training certificate, or a network router delivered to a branch office. The trouble is, none of these "firm deliverables" produce favorable outcomes in the previous examples.

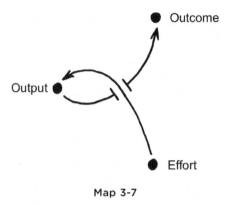

Map 3-7

It's a common trap to assume that outcomes are known and a mistake to place all emphasis on the outputs of work.

In many cases, we don't bother to carefully examine who or what a complex task directly affects. It's almost as if it was a grave secret that the HR policy is supposed to directly affect the employees, and that the analytics system will be used by the business app support team to help their business users, and that the office infrastructure initiative is aimed at benefiting the employees who work in that office. Except, there is no secrecy or conspiracy there at all. There's an inherent separation between the producer and the consumer. And this separation, for some reason, is something that everyone involved happens to feel comfortable with. But this is where it all begins: *understanding who or what is directly affected by your task.* It can be a person, a group of people or it can be an entity like an organization, for instance. Once this question has been answered and the affected parties are identified, here's the next one: *how exactly are they affected by the task?* Answering the second question grants us what we need: a proper understanding of outcomes.

It's not that these questions don't get answered because they are so hard to answer. The actual reason is that they are never really asked. And instead of focusing on those parties directly affected by the task, the focus is usually placed on those who oversee the execution – i.e. the bosses. As a result, the group of people responsible for the task execution has an entirely misplaced locus of impact: they care a lot about those who assess their outputs but do not focus on those who are supposed to benefit from the outcomes of their work. This profound discrepancy is very common and undermines complex initiatives involving changes in human behavior. A different approach is needed:

To succeed with a complex task that alters the way people act or think, empathy is required for those affected by the task.

Empathy is key to achieving outcomes, but also for formulating them in the first place. Most organizations and teams put so much effort in detailing out the outputs and relatively little effort into clarifying outcomes. They specify the requirements that determine the solution and they specify the design and effort involved – all of this accompanied by quite a bit of rigor and structure. And perhaps paradoxically, a single line of text is added to a separate column labeled "outcomes". And all such an outcome statement can do is provide the justification for the already planned (and maybe even committed to) effort. This is a fundamentally flawed approach that fosters organizational self-deception. Instead, outcomes should be an integral tool for understanding how the task should be progressing.

Retrofitting a formal outcome statement to an already decided-upon scope of work, without questioning that work, is a dangerous cultural scenario leading to the systemic justification of poor decisions. Instead, proper outcome analysis can and should trigger a change to the initially planned effort. This change sometimes can be very substantial.

Of course, it's best to plan complex initiatives in such a way that the planned effort which has no meaningful intended outcome, has no chance of being executed. And for that to happen, outcome analysis must be integrated from the very beginning, when the complex initiative is just being conceived. The reality, of course, is very different and your organization is likely to have scores of work items in their backlogs already, none of which contain a clearly defined outcome. And if that's the case, your primary goal will be to perform the required outcome analysis for those initiatives that the organization is ready to commit to in the near term.

Exploring Outcomes

What is a good outcome analysis? Here are the main aspects of a simple approach to get you started:

1 Identify the correct people to be involved. Good outcome analysis is the result of considering multiple, often divergent, points of view. Bring together those who define the task, those who execute it, and those who are affected by it. The different perspectives will mitigate confirmation bias.

2 Learn who or what is affected by the complex task. Find out who will directly benefit from the results of your work. Multiple categories of people and organizations might be involved.

3 Determine how each will be affected by the results of your work – that is the outcome you are looking for.

This is an exercise in *empathy* and is the only way to arrive at meaningful outcomes. Empathy is immersing ourselves in the mindset and activities of the people who will be affected by the complex task. Here's an example of a conversation that takes place during an outcome analysis session involving some team members and stakeholders:

Sergey (facilitator): "Guys, I would like you to pick a work item that, in your opinion, represents the highest importance."

Miesha (team stakeholder): "I suggest that we look into this one: 'CSR Knowledge Repository'."

Sergey: "Miesha, could you please describe what we intend to achieve with this item?"

Miesha: "Sure. The goal is to create a repository on the intranet that our customer service representatives (the CSRs) would use to familiarize themselves with various issues that the end consumer could be facing."

Sergey: "So, who is directly affected by this solution?"

Miesha: "Our customer service representatives."

Sergey: "And what exactly do I experience, as an affected person, in this case? Could you try to describe that for me?"

Miesha: "Well, a CSR will be able to browse through a broad, well-structured body of knowledge that contains the most relevant information about the product that the end consumer is buying. It also describes how they buy it, how it is delivered and set up, and so forth. It will provide a well-hyperlinked, WIKI-like interface with in-depth articles that will advance a CSR's knowledge on a broad variety of topics, making our customer service a world-class competitive—"

Sergey: "Miesha, my apologies for interrupting, but can I ask you to approach this slightly differently? Rather than describing what the affected person will experience, close your eyes and imagine that *you are* that person. Now, just describe what you see."

Miesha (pausing for a few moments): "I ... hmm ... When I get a customer call, I'll be more knowledgeable ..."

Veronica (a team member, one of the software developers): "I really wonder, when exactly are they going to find the time to do this?"

Sergey: "Do what, Veronica?"

Veronica: "To 'sit and browse' ..."

Vivek (another developer): "Good question! Besides ... even if they had the time, how should they read it? Where should they start and why? How should they progress through the information? If you told me that in order to learn Java (our programming language) I would have to read "Java Docs", I'd laugh at you. Not an optimal way to learn!"

Miesha: "What's Java Docs?"

Veronica: "It's a comprehensive knowledge repository for Java developers, like the one we intend to build for our CSRs. It contains deep, detailed articles, it has structure, and it's very helpful when you need to find a particular element of the Java programming language. But when you are not looking for something in particular, it's of little use. You won't just sit and go over a whole bunch of deep pages that are barely related to each other."

Miesha: "I think I understand. It's not the best way to learn, and we never even considered when they would have the time ..."

Veronica (closing her eyes): "What if, as a CSR, I could learn *during* the call? I receive a call and while the customer is describing the problem, I punch in some keywords and the system offers me a few possible, very short, articles describing a specific issue, and a possible recipe for fixing it."

Sergey took notes on the whiteboard.

Miesha: "How would you ensure that we have the right answers?"

Veronica: "We'd need to do a bit of homework, interview some CSRs, collect some typical issues. We'd basically have a continuously updated process to cover the most common consumer requests."

Sergey: "Feels like there's another affected person there, right?"

Veronica (nodding): "A content coordinator whose job is to maintain the knowledge base of the most relevant requests."

Sergey: "I think we've advanced our understanding quite a bit here, agreed?"

Miesha and the rest of the group nodded.

Sergey: "But so far these are hypotheses, and hypotheses need validation."

Miesha: "So, how do we validate?"

Vivek: "I'd talk to an actual CSR. See if any of it makes sense to them."

Sergey: "That would be a good first step."

Five minutes later a CSR, Kevin, was on the speakerphone, ready to answer the group's questions.

Kevin (after the ideas were described to him): "Could you give me an example of what a page would contain?"

Miesha: "Kevin, I thought you might be better positioned to

provide examples, as you deal with these issues on a daily basis. Or am I missing something?"

Kevin: "Well, okay, let's take one common issue. For example, the product configuration that was delivered doesn't satisfy the exact customer request. If you create a page for this issue, you need to be prepared to deal with multiple ambiguities involved in resolving the issue."

Miesha: "What kind of ambiguities?"

Kevin: "This issue can be raised for multiple different reasons. The customer might make a mistake in the product options they select while during the purchase. Or the customer might specify something in unclear terms and our guys in the shipping department interpret it incorrectly, then it ends up being not what they expected. Or maybe they specified correctly, but it was our error, to the same effect. All of these different scenarios resolve differently. There are also issues that can be solved either directly with the customer's help or by involving a Level-2 support person via a remote connection. And then—"

Miesha: "Are you saying we can't possibly provide all the answers?"

Kevin: "Generally speaking, no. Maybe for some issues. But some are so multifaceted that it is unrealistic."

Veronica: "What if instead of trying to answer and document all possibilities, we just answered a few of the most likely ones. And then the system could provide a reference to CSRs who have already encountered this type of issue and they might know more about it than me... I mean, the CSR who is currently searching for this problem in the knowledge repo."

Vivek: "You think that will work? If the problem can be caused by different factors, what if the CSR ends up contacting someone who has dealt with a different case?"

Kevin: "That's possible. But if someone has dealt with the issue, they know more than just their specific cause. They have a good idea of the systems involved, so it may be useful to chat with them, even if they haven't dealt with this precise issue. And they might point me in the right direction. And yes, sometimes it might not help, but if it's a common issue then it means that a number of CSRs have dealt with it, don't you think? And if someone doesn't know, I can ask the next person."

This process continues until the group has reached a certain level of understanding of the desired outcomes for different types of affected persons. Sergey captures it all on the board:

Outcomes for "CSR Knowledge Repository"	
CSR	Content Coordinator
• I am able to find answers to the top 20% consumer inquiries while on the call. • I see the names of the CSRs that have recently encountered the issue. If the steps suggested in the article don't help to resolve the customer issue, I can reach out to CSRs to learn how they dealt with it. • I can provide feedback on whether a particular page I used during the customer call helped to solve the problem, and what would be helpful to improve it. • I can submit a request on a missing topic if I encountered it multiple times, or when it's a high-impact customer problem.	• I can see feedback from CSRs on existing pages and the requests for the missing ones. • I can reach out to CSRs to see if anyone has additional input on particular entries that are missing or deficient.

Miesha (once Sergey finished the write-up): "Well, that's quite different from what was initially intended. I think we were overly focused on the repo itself. The goal, as I see it now, is to enable the right *behaviors* of the CSRs, and the content coordinators."

Sergey: "Excellent! But this isn't all of it, really."

Miesha: "Are we still missing something?"

Sergey: "Let's say we've done all of this work and somehow the solution we've built enables CSRs and Content Coordinators to do what we've just described. Then what? Why do we want them to be able to do all of this in the first place?"

Vivek: "Because we want to improve service quality for the customer?"

Miesha: "That's right!"

Sergey: "Could you please be more specific? What does that mean exactly?"

Vivek: "It means that the end consumer will have—"

Sergey: "Vivek, sorry to interrupt you, but try to use the same trick as before."

Vivek: "Oh, that's right." He closed his eyes and continued: "As an end customer, I get my problem solved quickly and effectively. I spend a short time on the phone with the CSR because they know how to solve my issue."

Sergey: "So, let me show what we have said to this point and draw a bigger picture view of our task."

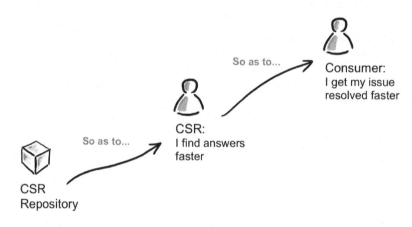

Map 3-8

Miesha: "You know what? Now that I'm looking at this picture, I'm not sure that this is what we really want."

Vivek: "Go on ..."

Miesha: "Yeah, so, it all sounds right. It sounds like we are building a tool that will make CSRs more efficient in finding the right answers, which in turn makes it easier for the customer to get their problem solved, but is that our ultimate outcome? I mean, we do all that to make the customer more satisfied, right?"

Vivek: "Certainly."

In the meantime, Sergey captured what had just been said:

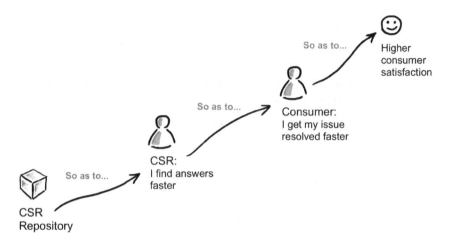

So as to... Higher consumer satisfaction

So as to... Consumer: I get my issue resolved faster

So as to... CSR: I find answers faster

So as to... CSR Repository

Map 3-9

Miesha (pointing at the updated diagram on the board): "If that's the case, what good does it do for us to keep resolving a recurring customer issue without addressing the root cause? There may be a problem in the description of the product they purchased, or in shipping, or with returns, but it seems all we do with this is just improve our ability to respond to issues, without truly examining *why* there is an issue in the first place. If we solved that issue, we'd reduce the volume of consumer calls, altogether."

Vivek: "Oh, I see. So, it's not even as much about CSRs—no offense, Kevin—as it is about the bigger picture view. A very effective CSR repository solution may be solving the wrong problem."

Kevin: "None taken. You guys are on the right track with this, as far as I'm concerned. I can tell you that some issues, even after being resolved, leave a really bad impression on our customers. Not everything can be remediated by good customer service. So, yes, some of these issues are hurting us quite a bit."

Miesha: "Exactly! A good repository solution would probably show some marginal improvement in the area of consumer satisfaction, luring us into pursuing it further, and essentially moving us in the wrong direction. It looks like a CSR repository is only a part of a more comprehensive solution."

Miesha realized that she needed to describe to her bosses what she had just learned, and start managing their expectations towards a more comprehensive solution. She was certain that the solution initially planned for would have been a waste of the company's time and money. A more thorough picture ultimately emerged:

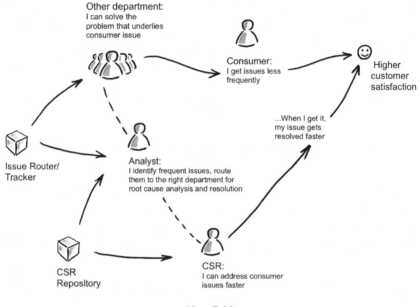

Map 3-10

The group concluded that while it makes sense to improve the service provided by CSRs, some routine analysis of frequent customer problems is needed, and a new role required. An analyst would look into frequently occurring issues and help route them within the organization, ultimately to someone who could help resolve the underlying problem. An Issue Routing and Tracking system would support the full cycle of identifying the root cause of a problem, resolving it, and verifying the solution. The end consumer satisfaction is expected to go up as a result of reducing the overall number of issues, and a better customer service experience would be rendered for those issues that still occur.

This example suggests a few important lessons about complex tasks:

1 Take a step back from outputs to see multiple levels of outcomes. For every node on the diagram, ask: "We do this, *so as to...* what?" This will help reveal the full *outcome chain*, not just the output and its immediate outcome.

2 Seeing a bigger picture—*a full outcome chain*—helps in spotting fundamental problems with solutions.

3 Empathy requires specificity. Enhance the understanding of outcomes by empathizing with those affected by the complex task. Different types of people are affected by the solution, just as there are different levels of outcomes.

4 Narrative, rather than a number, best describes the outcome of a complex task whenever the outcome involves a change in human behavior or in the thought process.

A Radical Departure From Legacy Thinking

When outcome analysis is performed as individual homework, there's nothing to prevent the traditional, output-dominated mindset from taking over, resulting in outcomes that are too generic to be useful, or are simply outputs labeled as outcomes. No one really intends to fail this exercise. The problem is that people don't know what a legitimate outcome looks or sounds like. Unfortunately, these people are often in charge of significant organizational capabilities geared towards achieving something great, at significant cost.

It is a good idea to run outcome analysis in the form of a workshop, a real-time, collaborative, well-facilitated effort akin to the interaction Miesha had with her group in the earlier example. A facilitator will help to keep everyone honest, and focused on actual outcomes and their proper enablement.

Just Defining Outcomes Is Not Enough

Outcomes need to be measured, not just defined. Here is an example that illustrates the importance of measuring outcomes:

An auto parts factory relies heavily on IT enablement for a multitude of processes in departments on and off the production floor. One IT team exists solely to provide improvements to such processes, making production and personnel more efficient. Every initiative this team executes goes through an outcome analysis process. The outcomes are expressed in very specific and tangible terms: the time saved for the factory personnel, as a result of using improved software systems. One such initiative might aim at saving 10,000 hours for the repair engineers over the course of a year. The problem is that nobody ever counts those saved hours once the solution is deployed. Initiatives are worked on, delivered by the team, and then it is simply *assumed* that the outcome has been achieved. Occasionally, after deployment, there are reports that a solution was dropped, perhaps because it caused personnel more trouble than the benefit provided. But beyond these extreme cases, no information flows back to the team in terms of how their solutions worked out. The team routinely finishes an initiative, hands the solution over to the deployment team, and hops over to the next initiative. And with each deployment, a checkbox appears on the team's board, signaling to them that they have "succeeded" with yet another initiative. They have collected dozens of such checkboxes, with hardly any solutions having been verified.

This example shows us that proper outcome focus cannot be achieved in an open-loop system. In a sense, the anticipated outcome of a complex task is no more than a hypothesis, and moving forward without validating the outcomes of previously executed tasks can lead to a tremendous amount of waste.

Why Do Organizations Obsess With Outputs and Not Outcomes?

Outcome focus is a challenge for individuals like you and me as well as for organizations. Here's a common example you, or someone you know, have experienced. I'm talking about going to the gym. Going to the gym consistently is a big deal, with many potential benefits, but it isn't clear at all if people are really benefiting from it. If you go to the gym and lift weights, you will gain strength over time, but if your original goal was weight loss, then you probably selected the wrong type of workout. You'd benefit from an endurance workout rather than weight lifting. The additional muscle mass from strength training may simply increase your overall weight without reducing body fat at all. There are multiple possible outcomes from going to the gym: losing extra weight, gaining strength, increasing muscle size, enhancing stamina, building confidence and self-esteem, relaxing after significant intellectual effort, reducing stress levels, to name a few. Each one of these requires its own approach and might expand beyond the gym experience itself, perhaps requiring a dietary change or an adjustment to your sleep pattern. Why do we refer to the whole activity as "going to the gym" as opposed to "gaining strength" or "improving stamina"?

In the same way, the initiative in the previous example was called "CSR repository" not "improving customer experience". We must learn to deal with the inattention to outcomes and the huge obsession with outputs and solutions. Organizations need a considerable discipline of thought to avoid the "solution obsession" and to follow through to proper outcome focus.

Human propensities are often amplified by certain organizational constructs and behaviors. Here are some reasons organizations might be pathologically inclined to favor outputs over outcomes:

Reason 1: Organizational Fragmentation

If the people involved in delivering a specific outcome belong to different departments, report to different bosses, or live and work on different continents, your organization is significantly *fragmented*. A fragmented organization leads to fragmented task execution, which means that each unit executes a particular part of the whole, but the units themselves don't interact with each other all that well. Each unit clearly understands their own part of the task, but not necessarily the overall outcome. Work is executed in a fragmented way but is also defined to best fit the fragmented structure of the organization. A huge amount of waste happens because the *way work is defined is far removed from its purpose*. The overlap between organizational units allows a view of the bigger picture. Teams organized in a fragmented way, around areas of expertise or parts of a solution, have very little overlap. Orchestration is required between fragmented teams, and this layer hijacks the link between the people doing the work and the outcomes that work is supposed to enable.

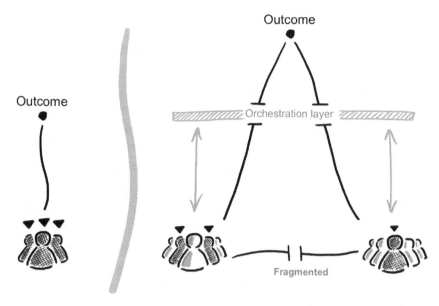

Map 3-11

Even with this high degree of fragmentation, the organization may believe its teams are collaborating well, simply because different departments are involved in building the solution. True collaboration means actually working side-by-side with each other, actively discussing further steps, frequently integrating the results of work, and routinely validating the outputs together to see if they are on the right track to achieving the outcomes.

Reason 2: Outcome Surrogates

An outcome description that is too vague and ill-defined becomes a surrogate for a true outcome. Anything can fit the profile of an overly generic outcome statement, which allows success to be claimed regardless of the actual outcomes. In Miesha's case, "higher customer satisfaction" is an example of an outcome surrogate. When Miesha's group realized "higher customer satisfaction" meant "fewer issues that are handled more effectively" there was sufficient clarity to inform better decisions.

Reason 3: Career Games

Aspiring to advance one's career is one thing, and systematically exploiting work for personal advancement is quite another. *It is always harder to achieve the right outcome than to produce outputs and declare victory based on that.* Tangible outputs can be reported or even demonstrated while completely failing to produce the right outcome. For example, a package of marketing materials may be taken as evidence of great achievement, while the associated marketing campaign fails to generate the right traction with potential consumers. In a similar way, a clever software product may be taken as the successful completion of an initiative, while the actual users reject it because it doesn't solve the real problem they are facing, even though the software functions well and has no obvious glitches.

Bosses often like tangible results so their subordinates quickly learn that focusing on outputs gives them an edge over their peers. This vicious cycle is produced by perfectly matched motivations on both sides. The only loser in this game is the organization itself.

Reason 4: Dysfunctional Funding

When the appetite for funding is higher than the available funds, organizational units may start looking for creative ways to improve their situation. In this case, it is natural to focus on outputs, as the amount of funding is often directly linked to the scope of work. Proper focus on outcomes may paradoxically be the least desirable effect an organizational unit wants to achieve.

Here are some examples of the underlying mechanisms in play:

1   A unit gets upper management approval to launch an initiative they've aspired to for a very long time. Now that they've obtained the line of funding, they will use it as if it was their last opportunity to also get various other things they've been wanting for quite a while. And so the funding package grows to include all the items on the wish list. Most of the package

now has nothing to do with achieving the correct outcomes, but it may also create damage far beyond just squandering the initial funding. The outputs are often assets that require further support, even though they may not represent any value whatsoever. For example, bloated software systems will incur significant technical debt and will routinely slow down any future enhancements, even though some of those enhancements may represent real value to the customer. Similarly, unnecessary marketing events will not only drain resources but will also require ongoing support in the form of follow-up activities.

2 A department serves various internal organizational units that bring initiatives along with the funding to execute them. The department is evaluated based on its ability to hit the originally estimated effort per initiative. The department was previously reprimanded for not meeting the allotted budget, so now they sandbag every time they produce estimations. But they also encourage their internal customers to request more scope as a part of their initiatives, including a broad variety of absolutely useless things. The greater the scope, the easier it is to balance the effort by carefully re-allocating costs across initiatives. All customers end up paying more, as the department systemically overestimates everything, and some customers end up subsidizing others without even knowing it. Again, scope is vital to playing this game and thus everyone becomes focused on outputs and not outcomes. The department wants as many initiatives as possible started at once, regardless of their available capacity, because more initiatives simply means more opportunity to re-allocate cost. Naturally, the group gets swamped in multi-tasking and lacks focus directed towards any particular initiative at any given time.

3 A unit underutilizing their funding may not get what they ask for in the next funding period, so completely useless work is initiated, purchases made or people hired, with the sole purpose of making sure the allocated funds are used up.

4   A large budget implies importance. The more funding you get, the more successful you think you are, and the more attention your boss will give you. The definition phase of a project involves lots of scoping decisions, and many internal customers will think this is their chance to get the things they have so long desired. Cutting off things of questionable value would eliminate waste, but reducing the budget reduces the exposure our project manager seeks for their career advancement.

These examples have one thing in common: the outputs are geared towards securing more funding rather than producing better outcomes. The reasons vary, but the desire for funding pulls attention away from outcomes:

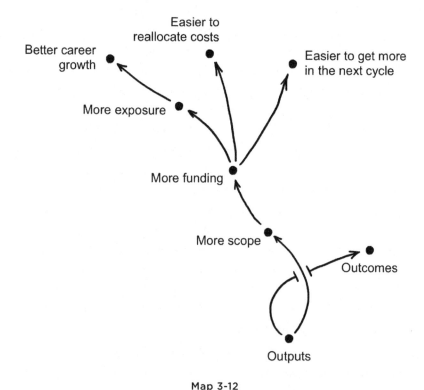

Map 3-12

Outcome focus delivers real value to the company, rather than focusing on personal career goals or the tribal needs of a particular department.

The fundamental problem is that the people who decide upon and enforce organizational funding policies are often removed from outcomes. To them, funding policies that are tied to scope—and thus outputs—are a good thing. They are unable to see the dark side of it, because in order to see it, they would have to keep an eye on the outcomes – which is ultimately the only thing that suffers at the end of the day.

Reason 5: The Inherent Complexity of Outcome Enablement

Intangible outcomes can complicate the outcome focus.

Two good examples of complex tasks with intangible outcomes are, Task A: improve employee satisfaction, and Task B: increase the usability of a software product.

What does "employee satisfaction" mean? Does it mean that employees say they are more satisfied? People often say what they are expected to say, especially when it is unsafe to say how they really feel. For one person, satisfaction might come from being uninterrupted in their routine, while another might be satisfied by challenges and opportunities to learn. Many different aspects might be relevant to the outcome of Task A.

The situation with Task B is very similar. Does "good usability" mean that customers enjoy using the product? Or that they can effectively perform routine tasks? And what does "effectively performing a task" mean anyway? Maybe an application helps an accountant finish their tasks quickly, or brings their attention to important nuances, slowing down their work but improving it?

Generally speaking, intangible outcomes are often much better described with a *deep narrative* as opposed to a simplistic numerical indicator. Intangible outcomes have their own *structure* and most organizations fail to discover that structure.

Reason 6: Fear

Outcome focus may reveal large amounts of waste, various pet projects, horrendous funding inefficiencies, bad decisions, and other dysfunctions in an organization, and it can take real courage to raise your voice and start pointing them out. Those with the determination to push an organization in the right direction by pursuing outcomes understand how tough and rewarding, this can be. Maybe you are one of them?

Reason 7: Command-and-Control Culture

In a command-and-control environment, weak signals from the bottom of the organization are filtered on their way up the organization and suppressed at each level of the hierarchy. The enterprise is unable to make adjustments, even when some people realize that the current course of action will lead to an unfavorable outcome. Command-and-control culture fosters rigidity and inertia: exactly the opposite is needed for successful outcome focus.

Signs That Your Organization Obsesses With Outputs

Any of the following signs might indicate an organization favors outputs instead of outcomes.

Scope and Time Are Used as Primary Success Indicators

Look at the main variables that are routinely discussed when it comes to the status of initiatives in your organization. If what you mostly hear is "scope" and "time", if the conversations are usually about "what has already been implemented?" and "how long it will take to do the rest?", it is very likely that your organization lacks proper focus on the outcomes of their effort. There is a pretty clear reason why scope and time can so easily become the primary "success indicators". On one hand, outcome focus is no trivial matter, and organizations that have habitually neglected outcomes throughout their existence can't change their instincts overnight and suddenly become outcome-focused. On the other hand, there is always a strong natural propensity towards control among leaders. And to control an initiative, one needs progress indicators: seeing good progression in task execution creates a very comforting feeling. And however misleading they may be, scope and time happen to be very convenient indicators. They are easy to capture and are universally applicable to any complex initiative, simply because any work has a scope and it progresses through time. No wonder various theories have been built around managing task execution based on these two parameters. People are trained and certified in various methodologies based on scope and time as the primary measures of progress. It usually doesn't even occur to organizations that those indicators have nothing to do with real progression on the task. Organizations readily and fluently speak the language of scope and time because it scales so well. Nothing could be easier! No need to mess with contextual indicators that, in fact, may have their own complicated structure that needs to be discovered and properly comprehended. No need to bother figuring out whether the initiative is going to make the correct impact. Instead, when the question is asked whether the initiative was successful, a typical answer sounds like this: "We finished the project in the intended scope and within the time boundary, right? So, it was successful."

Everything appears to get so much easier with scope and time. And yet scope and time are the *most* deceiving indicators when it comes to tasks of complexity. Managing a complex initiative based on scope and time is a little like judging a person's character based on their weight and height.

Everything Is a Success

How many initiatives or projects does your organization officially regard as a lesson on how *not* to execute a complex task? If nothing comes to mind, your organization might care more about politics than about actually succeeding with their effort. This tendency can grow deep into the organizational culture and entirely govern organizational behavior.

The organization may well recognize the problem at some level: even though "everything is a success", there are some "successes" that people prefer not to talk about.

Nobody Can Tell How it Really Worked Out

What was the effectiveness of the solution delivered? What impact was made? Were favorable outcomes achieved? Common answers might be that everything was executed successfully, or that the customer reviewed it positively, or that no one has complained about it yet. More precise responses like "I guess somebody measures that, but my department wouldn't know" or "There is a standard process for measuring achieved value" don't actually answer the original questions either, because no one knows if there was any value for the effort they delivered. This is a clear indication of a disconnect between effort and outcomes.

Outcome Chains and Outcome Ownership

There are all kinds of outputs within an organization: software and IT assets, marketing materials, commercial data, business process descriptions and guardrails, policies, strategy documents, training materials, and so on and so forth. And each output usually has an owner, whose responsibility it is to deliver, update, or maintain those assets. Their performance is typically measured based on how well they manage those assets.

What you won't be able to find very easily are *outcome owners*. The only common outcome owners that are reliably present in organizations are the leaders with profit and loss (P&L) responsibility. However, they are usually significantly removed from lower-level outcomes. As a result, there is effectively no outcome ownership. The lack of ownership over those lower-level outcomes leads to enormous amounts of waste which snowballs along the outcome chain, level by level. Here's a simple example:

An HR team wants to help employees of a software development organization acquire new abilities in addition to their main expertise area. This is called T-shaping, where the vertical line of the letter "T" represents the significant depth of knowledge in one area, and the horizontal line represents some practical understanding in other areas. T-shaping can have a pretty powerful economic impact. People with broader skill-sets can organize around new work more effectively and deliver systems to business users faster. Business users will be able to execute their business scenarios which leads to additional revenue for the business. So far so good:

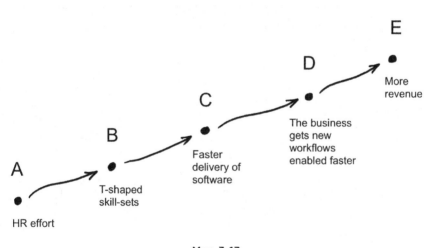

Map 3-13

This is our *outcome chain*. Node "A" represents outputs or the effort invested in the task. Node "B" is the immediate outcome of that effort. Nodes C-E are higher-order outcomes. Let's say George, VP of Customer Success, owns the profit and loss responsibility for customer services. He, therefore, owns node "E" as the ultimate outcome of producing higher service revenue for the organization. The various outputs along the chain (training organized by HR, software delivered by the teams, and business process guidelines devised by process engineers) also have owners. The problem is that *outcomes B, C, and D are not really owned by anyone*. The HR team partners with the development organization to coordinate some training for developers, but this training doesn't make anyone T-shaped. To enable T-shaping, people need to be motivated to expand their skill-set, which in this particular organization is not the case. They also need to be immersed in an environment where they can pair with professionals and learn practical aspects through direct observation and interaction. They need to advance their understanding of the organizational ecosystem and the consequences of their actions. Formal training is just a fraction of what is required, so no wonder it fails to deliver on its promise. The problem cascades all the way to node "E" making George furious and eager to find out whose fault it is that his high-order outcome wasn't delivered.

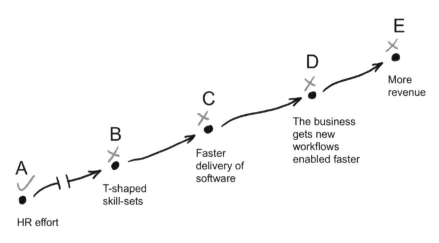

Map 3-14

HR and the leaders of the development organization proudly report that they've sent all their people to training, using most of the training budget, proving that they have done their part and that the problem cannot be with T-shaping. The search for the culprit shifts elsewhere on the outcome chain, but no one asks whether any of the software team members have applied their newly acquired skill-sets. Why not? The answer is simply that nobody owned that outcome and thus nobody really kept the outcome in their sights. Nobody bothered to think about what evidence of a successful outcome would look like.

But it gets even more complicated than that in long outcome chains like the one in our example. Assume that outcome "B" was actually achieved, meaning that there was some success in T-shaping. But what really happened is that the newly acquired skills generally duplicated the skills that were abundantly available anyway. And it happened quite naturally this way. People who had bottlenecked skills were busy all the time, and so couldn't provide much guidance to those seeking to expand their skill-sets. The result of such T-shaping is pretty much the same as no T-shaping: the next node in the outcome chain is not properly enabled because the wrong outcome has been achieved.

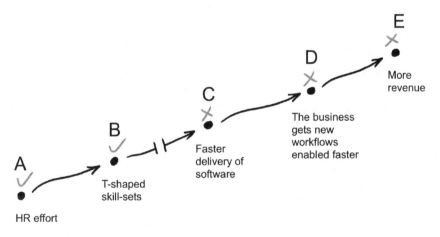

Map 3-15

It is only useful to pursue T-shaping on certain sets of skills that are in high demand.

If we say that T-shaping happened on the correct skill-sets, in other words, that outcome "B" was successfully achieved, this would allow faster delivery, so outcome "C" was also achieved, but the software systems were defined poorly, so all that has actually been accomplished is that the group managed to speed up delivery of ineffective, unusable software. Outcome "D" is still missing, and outcome "E" is still in jeopardy.

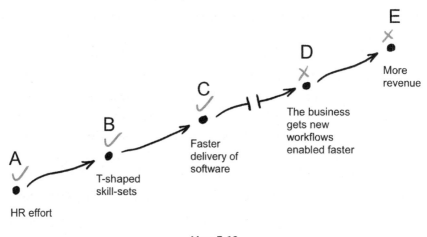

Map 3-16

But even if we assume that the software was done right, and so "D" was delivered, there is no guarantee that the desired new business workflows actually make sense, so the ultimate outcome is still not delivered.

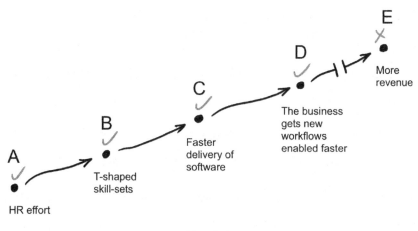

Map 3-17

To succeed with the ultimate outcome, all lower-level outcomes need to have owners who hold responsibility for the outcomes, not outputs. A disconnect anywhere in the outcome chain easily jeopardizes the ultimate outcome of the task.

An outcome owner can be anyone with sufficient authority to direct the outputs in any way that enables better outcomes. *It doesn't need to be a single person* and could be taken on by a group of people sharing different aspects of outcome ownership. Here's a high-level description of the outcome owner role:

Outcome Owner
Preconditions
Outcome owners must not be incentivized on the basis of produced outputs as their primary responsibility is delivering outcomes.
This does not imply, however, that they should necessarily be subjected to an outcome-based incentive model. In complex tasks, there often is significant uncertainty associated with outcomes, and thus careful treatment should be applied here.
Impediments to proper outcome focus should be carefully analyzed and acted upon. Creating an outcome owner will not solve a problem if the rest of the system remains fundamentally averse to outcome focus.

Outcome Owner
Responsibilities
Ensure a proper definition of outcomes by discovering immediate outcomes as well as a bigger picture view of the entire outcome chain.
Establish a way to obtain evidence of achieving the outcome with both quantitative and qualitative measures, usually highly contextual.
Align everyone involved in achieving the outcome to the idea of the outcome.
Ensure a mechanism for adjusting outputs in order to gain better outcomes, watching closely for signs of obsession with outputs.
Establish mechanisms to learn whether the flow of task execution is heading toward favorable outcomes.
Continually refine the understanding of outcomes as new facts emerge, managing stakeholders' expectations accordingly.

Applying this role definition to our example, it's clear the owner of outcome "B" should not be held responsible for training. This person should *actually* be held responsible for whether the proper T-shaping happened.

In most organizational environments, an outcome owner is the most overlooked role at different levels, even though this role can glue together different links of the outcome chain. The cost of not having an outcome owner is immense!

To establish outcome owner roles in your organization, keep in mind the preconditions in the table above, especially with identifying and acting on impediments to a proper outcome focus. Some examples of impediments were listed in the section "Why Organizations Are Obsessing with Outputs and Not Outcomes", earlier in this chapter. But there are plenty more things that may make it impossible for the outcome owner to properly do their job. An outcome owner with a boss incentivized to deliver outputs will not be able to do their job without constant conflict with that boss's primary career objective. That's a pretty unfavorable situation and just one example of why it is so important to establish the right environment for outcome ownership.

Later in this book, we will refine our understanding of this role with respect to various vital aspects of a complex task.

We will also be referring to the notion of outcome chains on multiple occasions in future chapters, as it is one of the key tools to acquire a holistic view of an enterprise's value creation.

Outcome chains define a structured value system for the organization. Failure to understand the outcome chain leads to large amounts of waste. Optimizing outcome chains is synonymous with optimizing the organization.

Outcomes Emerge Rather Than Are Created

Complex environments are full of uncertainty and ambiguity. These are common conditions when so much depends on human interpretation, judgment, motivation, and other powerful and intangible forces. These forces don't follow exact trajectories, so it is difficult to predict all possible outcomes, their likelihood, and their impacts. Given the inherently incomplete knowledge, a *range* of possible outcomes is a much more reasonable paradigm than a specific outcome. In fact, some of the outcomes in the range may not be even known.

But in the previous exercise, we did the exact opposite of this: we tried to describe the *specific* experiences of a person affected by the task. There is a compelling reason for that. Organizations and teams can be so far removed from outcomes that deep empathy is the only chance to "reconnect" with outcomes, and empathy requires specificity. The output bias is so strong that by "pretending" the outcome is a "dot" rather than a "range", you have a chance to cross the chasm from outputs to outcomes. Once an understanding has been established, the next step is to learn about the multiple possible outcomes and how to navigate to the right one.

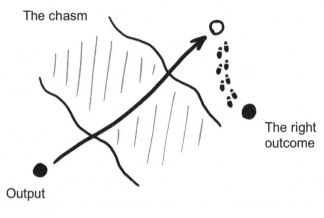

Map 3-18

And if the chasm is not crossed, an awareness of multiple possible outcomes is pointless. In other words: "hop" over the chasm first and then "walk" to the correct destination on the other side.

Empathy is a powerful learning tool and an effective shortcut to understanding outcomes but is only achieved through specificity, and that warrants a caution: the actual outcomes of complex tasks are emergent in nature. Thinking about and analyzing outcomes, rather than getting stuck with outputs, is helpful but should not give you the illusion of locking onto an exact outcome statement.

It is so important to manage expectations because organizations love to lock onto a specific "dot", instead of a "range", and that "dot" may easily be considered a commitment, causing serious problems later on. In complex tasks, the idea of the outcome is constantly refined, as progress in the task unveils new and important lessons about the environment.

Chapter 6 will be devoted to the subject of emergence in much greater depth.

When Outcomes Are Clearly Known

Organizations and teams will sometimes know the outcomes reliably. When the objective of a complex task is to repair a system or a process that worked before and now doesn't, we know precisely what behavior we are looking for and that it needs to be fixed. In this case, most of the complexity lies in diagnosing the problem, addressing the underlying causes of the issue, and making it work again, so the lack of understanding of outcomes is not an issue here.

But a potential pitfall is that organizations are extremely prone to believe that they "know" the expected behavior of a system or a process, even one that has not been created yet. Everything appears "obvious" and "reliably known" upfront, but this is generally an illusion.

Collateral Outcomes

A desired outcome is one that we expect to be beneficial, but the environment can be so complex, manifesting unpredictable behaviors, that other different types of outcomes appear. These outcomes can be difficult to spot but may be decisive to the organization's success or failure. We will call them *collateral outcomes*, in contrast to the *primary outcomes* that are the main purpose of the task. Here are a few examples of collateral outcomes:

1   The primary outcome of developing an enterprise application is enabling some business processes. But over time, under the pressure of deadlines and poor attention to technical detail, the application architecture deteriorates to the point where adding any new functionality becomes dangerous as well as difficult. This phenomenon is commonly referred to as "technical debt". And when a significant amount of such debt accumulates, it is very hard to pay off. Technical debt is an example of a bad collateral outcome, but collateral outcomes don't have to be

bad. In fact, technical debt's opposite, a healthy codebase, is also a collateral outcome, just a less common one.

2 A marketing campaign aims at the primary outcome of converting more customers. The way the conversion is achieved ultimately makes customers feel like they're being taken advantage of, and they become a lot harder to retain in the long run. Conversion has been successfully achieved but at the cost of customer loyalty. This decreased customer loyalty is a collateral outcome.

Primary outcomes are the reason an initiative gets funding in the first place, and are usually more visible, more tangible than collateral outcomes. Collateral outcomes might not be noticed until it is too late, or might even be intentionally ignored. Collateral outcomes are often delayed in time, as a result of a cumulative effect that accrues over time. There can be many collateral outcomes:

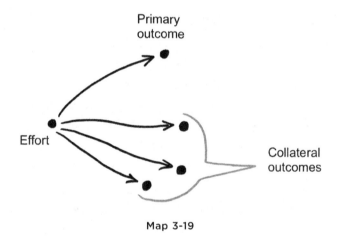

Map 3-19

In the case of a software application, another example of a collateral outcome might be poor usability of the system. In the case of the marketing campaign, the company has negatively impacted customer loyalty, but also unintentionally triggered a different behavior in the market. The competition rushes to exploit the blunder, gearing their marketing campaigns to expose the weak value proposition of the company and offering a stronger, competing message to the same customer base.

The examples in this section demonstrate why collateral outcomes may significantly affect the outcome chain, and sometimes even inhibit the achievement of the immediate primary outcome (or the building of the outputs):

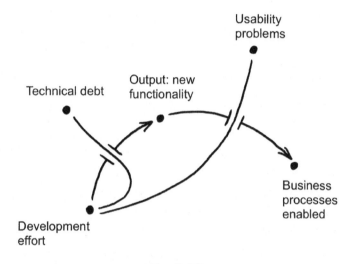

Map 3-20

Sometimes a collateral outcome may *not* have a direct impact on the immediate outcome, but instead ends up having a significant influence on higher-order outcomes further out in the outcome chain:

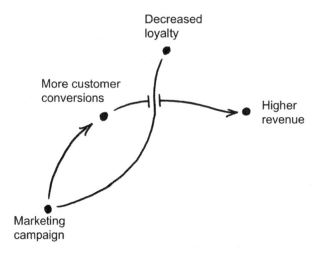

Map 3-21

Identifying collateral outcomes is a hard task, but not an impossible one. The usual problem is that organizations don't have an established communication mechanism to propagate the signal from those who can see the early signs of collateral outcomes, to those that are empowered to make appropriate decisions. In a command-and-control environment, people may not even feel safe enough to raise an issue like the one above, where customers are being acquired through a campaign but are then inactive. Even if a collateral outcome is identified and communicated early enough, it still might not be addressed. The incentive structure in the organization is one possible reason. Hardly any manager will be interested in investing in technical debt reduction if their performance is primarily evaluated based on the amount of new functionality delivered. The problem gets exacerbated by the *discontinuity of responsibility* – a side-effect that occurs when organizations frequently move people around. As a result, nobody suffers consequences of their actions, everybody ignores longer-term negative effects, simply because they are not the ones who are going to deal with them. Collateral outcomes in this case spin out of control, inflicting delayed yet powerful damage to the organization.

The outcome owner must keep an eye open for potential collateral outcomes. Part of this responsibility lies in ensuring effective interactions between levels of the organization, but especially in fostering bottom-up feedback.

Preventive Outcomes

Outcomes that are *preventive* in nature require special treatment. Instead of enabling certain behaviors, a preventive outcome makes them impossible. Preventive outcomes are often high-impact qualities such as safety, security, reliability, and so forth. Safety means preventing incidents that may endanger certain individuals, groups, or entire ecosystems. Security means preventing the harmful activities of hostile forces. Reliability means preventing unwanted downtime of a service. Here we are talking about *undesired* behaviors that the outcome must prevent, in contrast to the *desired* behaviors in the previous section.

Because of this distinction, the methods we've previously considered for analyzing regular outcomes need a crucial modification to make them work: an *inversion*. Inversion means that instead of seeking what enables the outcome, we're looking for factors and conditions that would jeopardize the outcome. We need to analyze what scenarios would make the environment unsafe, or insecure, or unreliable. Empathy can be leveraged too, but a delicate approach is needed. We are no longer trying to empathize with those who will benefit from the preventive outcome, but rather with an explicit or implicit adversary. To conduct a useful analysis of a preventive outcome, we need to adopt the mindset of an adversary. An adversary is *explicit* when an actual person or group of people potentially exists who could benefit from jeopardizing your desired outcome. If they do not exist, we say that the adversary is *implicit* and in this case, we empathize with an artificial construct. Security has an explicit adversary, while safety and reliability do not, and so introducing an implicit adversary facilitates the analysis. Inversion can be considered a constructive application of the principle that *it takes a thief to catch a thief.*

To have effective cyber-security as an outcome, for example, you must be able to empathize with the hacker. This type of empathy will reveal vulnerabilities in the enterprise's IT landscape, and how to exploit them. A blunt "install-this-firewall-software" approach doesn't work in complex or high-stakes situations. But empathy with the hacker may reveal cross-domain breach opportunities: perhaps by combining social engineering and the exploitation of technology vulnerabilities, the adversary can seize control of critical IT assets.

In case of reliability, there is no actual adversary, but we will nevertheless invent and artificially create a "person" that can manipulate the conditions of the environment to jeopardize the desired outcome, and cause interruptions in the service. An imagined adversary may help us to spot scenarios capable of interrupting the normal operations of the system, which would only happen randomly under normal conditions.

The inversion method seems simple, but preventive outcomes are inherently complex. To get started with regular outcomes, it is enough to find one productive scenario leading to success, but with preventive outcomes, it's the other way around: it just takes one productive scenario for a cyber-attack to succeed in causing havoc. Your defense is to search for *various* scenarios that could lead to failure. Finding all such scenarios is practically unfeasible, so regardless of how good your analysis was, there remains a high degree of uncertainty about the potential of an unexpected attack using a novel approach. This is exactly what happens with a zero-day cyber-attack, which exploits an unknown or unaddressed vulnerability for which there is no known remedy.

Preventive outcomes can be compound in nature, with multiple crucial aspects beyond just preventing undesired scenarios, perhaps including recovery in case of adverse scenario, notifications, emergency procedures, and so on.

Although it might not be obvious, preventive outcomes are often a part of regular business outcomes. A business outcome rarely involves doing something in isolation. Achieving favorable outcomes is a result of gaining an advantage over the competition. The desire to prevent a competitor from succeeding automatically introduces a preventive outcome and benefits from inversion analysis, with the competitor is the adversary: competitor empathy being a primary tool.

The Right Instinct

By focusing on outcomes a culture can arise where nothing is automatically good or useful simply because it is expected, or because the boss says so. The instinct behind outcomes drives organizational behavior towards critical thinking and towards empirical validation of decisions. It offers a rare chance to focus more on creating business value and to spend less time playing organizational politics.

🎎 Taking Action

1   Identify outcomes for the complex task (project or initiative) you are a part of. Use recommendations from the "Exploring Outcomes" section of this chapter. The goal is to get to a detailed, meaningful first-person outcome narrative. This empathy exercise enables you, as a *producer*, to embrace the mindset of the *consumer* of your work.

2   Make certain the outcome is truly an outcome and not just an output in disguise. Your task's purpose will likely enable some human behavior (inside or outside of your enterprise) and this behavior is probably the outcome you are looking for. Don't let your outcome state something like "create software or features or policies or guidelines or descriptions" as these are all outputs and not outcomes. Human behavior is most likely your immediate outcome!

3   Validate the outcome narrative with the people your outputs will affect. Talk to them. Show them your outcome narrative, or develop a narrative with them and compare it to your initial version.

4   Determine who will be the Outcome Owner in your environment. If it is you, start working to embrace the key responsibilities of the Outcome Owner described in this chapter. If it isn't you, help identify that person and help them to adopt the Outcome Owner responsibilities. Either way, it is your job to demonstrate leadership by establishing clear outcome ownership in your environment.

CHAPTER 4

The Science and the Art of Probing

Unknown Answers to Unknown Questions

Meet Bob. Bob has been a plumber for over a decade and is co-owner of the business. His current job is a clogged kitchen sink. First of all, he goes to the basement and examines the network of exposed pipes. Then he comes back upstairs, turns on the water in different parts of the house, and watches where the water drains well and where it doesn't. In just a few minutes he learns that the congestion is not actually in the kitchen sink, but somewhere further down the main sewer line. And that's enough information for him to take action. He brings a drill snake from his van. In about five minutes the water drains perfectly well in every sink in the house. The customer is highly satisfied with the service.

Meet Ashley. Ashley is an HR director in a 2000-employee company. Ashley is dealing with a different kind of clogged system. The lack of skills of the employees is impeding the productivity of her organization. The company has a long history of under-developed skills as a result of a cost-saving mentality, while the actual tasks have become more complex. The company's leadership finally had to pay attention to the accumulated "skill debt". Ashley was tasked with growing the workforce's skill level at any cost. After comprehensive interviews, Ashley and her team determined what skills were missing and where. Some employees were sent to public training courses, and other training organizations were invited to train employees onsite. But productivity didn't improve, and attrition went up. The more capable employees mastered new skills and promptly left the company, while those who stayed generally showed little progress. Despite the expense of training, the "skill debt" was unchanged, and the company had lost some talented people.

Why do we have success in one case and failure in the other?

To answer the question we need to take a deeper look at both tasks.

You have probably noticed that both tasks were undertaken with some important bits of information missing: in Bob's case, it wasn't clear exactly where the pipes were clogged. And in Ashley's task, it was unclear exactly what skills were missing. Both people performed an additional action—*probing*—to find the missing information. The difference? In Bob's case, the probing he did was fully sufficient to effectively accomplish the task – in Ashley's case, it clearly wasn't. But what's even more interesting is that Ashley and her team assumed that the information they had acquired would be sufficient to succeed with the task. Bob knew all the variables involved and only needed to find the values for those variables. Ashley, on the other hand, didn't know all the variables that governed her task and subsequently, the outcome caught her completely by surprise. In other words, Bob was aware of the unknowns in his task (and therefore we can call those *known unknowns*) while Ashley wasn't aware of all the unknowns in her case (and so had to deal with *unknown unknowns*).

Could Ashley have approached her task better? Could she have probed for some other variables, foreseen the attrition problem, and changed the plan?

Unlikely. Here's why...

In addition to Ashley's company (Company A), consider the results seen by other companies with significant skill debt. Company B resorted to a similar training program as Ashley's but actually succeeded. The skills improved, but attrition didn't increase. For Company C, nobody left the organization, but the training did not lead to any improvement in skills. Why would outcomes differ across the three companies? The employees at Ashley's company felt pressured and under-appreciated, so free training was seen merely as a tool to improve their chances in the job market. At Company B, leadership was generally supportive and sensitive to employees' needs, so employees saw an opportunity to advance at a company they already enjoyed being a part of. In company C, although people had a good compensation package and solid potential career growth, any mistake counted against the employee. It's impossible to learn a new skill without making a mistake, so there was no incentive to apply anything learned from training because of the risk of jeopardizing their careers. And any other organization might have a distinct outcome and their own reasons why those outcomes occurred. So it was not Ashley's fault that she did not know all her variables upfront, as Bob did. Bob's task was simpler, and Ashley was dealing with an *inherently complex task*.

Complex tasks depend on too many variables. Probing for known unknowns is not enough to reliably predict outcomes. Complex tasks always contain unknown unknowns with a significant impact on the task outcome.

If we think of the mental model of a task as a "territory map", then for simpler tasks you would see:

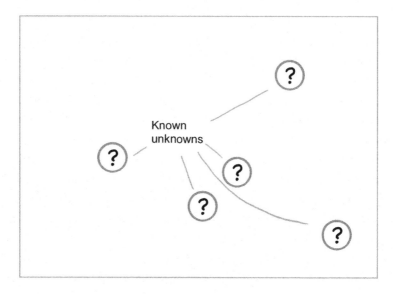

Map 4-1

You can see the entire map except for certain areas where you have to probe to find out the missing information. For inherently complex tasks, the situation looks quite different:

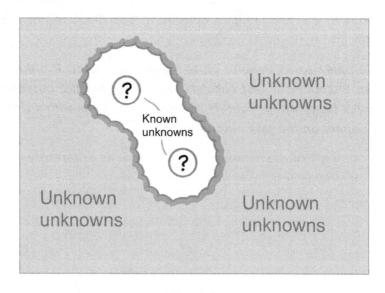

Map 4-2

Here, only a *part* of the "territory" is mapped out. The rest is "not yet explored" and there is no way to say how many or what kind of unknowns exist outside the visible area.

This explains why a simple checklist is not enough to guarantee success with a complex task, and neither is expertise. Both checklists and experts can be useful, but neither is enough to succeed because they can help only with known unknowns.

So, what's needed to help uncover the missing piece of the puzzle – the unknown unknowns? The answer is surprisingly simple: just like with known unknowns, this type of discovery also requires probing. Only unlike in Bob's case where we probed to get missing values of the known variables, here we probe to actually discover the variables themselves.

Next, we are going to explore some specific ways of probing for unknown unknowns. But before we do that, we must bring in an important notion: the *system* associated with the task. The system is the environment where the task is executed and includes any aspect that influences the success of the outcome. Systems can have many aspects, including the people working on the task, the people affected by it, various types of material resources, intangible assets, and so on. Bob's system consists of Bob himself, the homeowner, and the plumbing in the house. Bob executes his task in familiar territory with a successful outcome. Ashley's system includes employees, their supervisors, skills, and training. When the system is straightforward, the task is simple. When the system is hard to figure out, the task becomes more difficult, and we refer to both the system and the task as *complex*. In complex systems, it might not be clear where the boundaries of the system lie, so it is difficult to know whether you have explored as much as you need to. Finding the boundary of the territory is an important part of understanding the environment and figuring out the system. For example, in Ashley's system, it wasn't immediately clear that the job market was also a part of the system. It nevertheless ultimately transpired that training impacted retention of the workforce.

Direct vs. Indirect Probing

The problem with probing for unknown unknowns is that we don't know exactly what we are looking for. So what *do* we know? We know that we have to:

1 "Stir up" the system to make it reveal its nature

2 Pay attention to all signals

Be careful that your expectations don't limit what signals you see. When we direct our perception toward something in particular, we narrow our focus and overlook important facts that lie beyond.

One simple and obvious way Ashley could probe for unknown unknowns is by picking a subset of employees and sending them to training, and then watching whatever happens after. A spike in attrition could have been discovered using this approach (of course, subject to properly selecting the subset of employees and training course, as well as giving the experiment a sufficient runtime).

This is an example of *direct probing*. Direct probing works as follows. Let's say we have an overall plan of how to execute our task. (Of course, we must keep in mind that this plan is entirely hypothetical and that our probing is in fact going to help us prove or disprove its validity.) Having a plan of attack implies that we already know what enablers we will have to put in place to achieve the desired outcome.

Plan of intent:

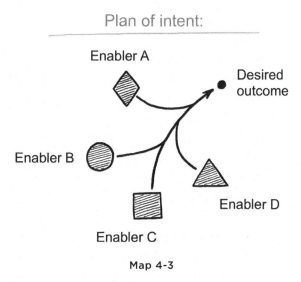

Map 4-3

(The key enabler in Ashley's task would be "to train all people".)
Implementing enablers in full would take up time and financial
resources, and if we didn't get the desired outcome, it would all be
a waste. A smarter, faster, and cheaper way would be to approximate the enablers instead. This is the idea behind direct probing:
we *directly* follow the existing idea of the solution.

Approximation:

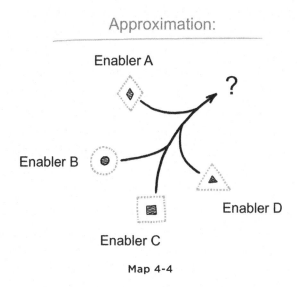

Map 4-4

(For Ashley, an approximation of the enabler "to train all people" is to instead have *some* people attend *some* training courses.)

If the approximation is good, the system will respond to direct probing in a similar way to full execution of the task. We will learn much sooner if something is wrong with the plan, at a lower cost, and with less damage. Best of all, we will be able to adjust the plan and continue. Ashley could have used a pilot of just 100 people as a fair approximation of the full task.

The approximation can be achieved by executing the task in a limited way, or on a smaller scale. If we were building a software system, we could deliver a system with limited features to a sample of likely users. If we launched a marketing campaign, we could show a subset of the ads to a test audience.

This type of probing not only provides vital information but can also incrementally advance us in terms of the task execution. But not all the tasks allow for such luxury. Sometimes in order to do direct probing, a different type of activities is required. And those activities really do only one thing: provide important information (although they do not directly advance the task execution itself). One example of this would be building a hardware system. Whereas in software a quick "increment" can often be built, delivered, and then, possibly, further adjusted and enhanced towards a complete solution, with hardware, direct probing would rather assume creating a prototype. The prototype would certainly help us learn important things, but would most likely end up discarded. And so we arrive at two subtypes of direct probing: *incremental*, where probing facilitates discovery, and also directly advances the execution of the task; and *non-incremental*, where probing produces new information but does not directly advance the task execution. Non-incremental probing should not be seen as a bad thing because in many cases it is the only kind of probing possible.

But however useful, direct probing (including both incremental and non-incremental techniques) has its limitations, as some outcomes are really hard to approximate in principle. This happens when:

- The outcome is not immediately affected by the task effort, but rather has to emerge over time. This happens when the goal of the task is to develop new habits in a group of people or to grow a new mindset. An example from Chapter 3 was a quality improvement program that involved changing the way people think and act across the organization. The program was a failure because the emergent nature of habit and mindset was not taken into account. The task was instead treated in a mechanistic way, assuming that the desired outcome could be "designed" by defining processes and practices in a top-down manner.

- The outcome depends on preconditions only available in the full execution of the task, and cannot be approximated by providing any partial solution. Preparing an organization for a compliance-related audit or certification, or working to launch a fund-raising event or a trade show are examples of this.

- We don't have any particular plan of action. Not having a plan of action is actually not as bad as it sounds. In fact, it is often far better than having a bogus plan, but believing that it's great – a circumstance too many organizations habitually fall into. When there's no clear idea of *what* to approximate as a desired future state, approximation is clearly inapplicable.

A different approach is needed in such cases, one that is *indirect* with respect to the solution. In *indirect probing*, we don't probe by approximating the solution. Instead, we find an alternative way to tap into the system's forces that the solution is supposed to interact with or leverage.

Ashley could use indirect probing effectively by interviewing former employees about the training program. Although this sounds strange at first, consider that a current employee intending to leave would be unlikely to tell their employer about it. A former employee, however, has already played their hand, and they are much more likely to be open in their responses.

Designing indirect probing scenarios requires some creativity and an open-minded attitude. Some basic indirect scenarios can be built by using simple constructive methods, such as *the Substitution Method*. At its core, it is very simple. Start by taking inventory of the key components in your system. Ashley's key components are:

- Employees
- Training courses
- Skills

For every component, we want to find substitutes that can "interact" with the rest of the system. A possible substitute for the "employees" component could be "former employees", "future employees", or "employees of other organizations". Instead of "training", we might consider "learning by doing", "reading an article", or "magically acquiring a skill" some other way. And the substitutes for "skills" could be "formal credentials" or "unneeded skills" (skills not needed by the organization). We summarize these substitutes in a table:

Components	Employees	Training courses	Skills
Alternatives	Former employees	Learning by doing	Formal credentials
	Future employees	Reading an article	Unneeded skills
	Employees of other companies	Magically acquiring a skill	

We can use this table now to construct different probing scenarios by choosing different options from the three columns. One scenario could be the following combination:

Components	Employees	Training courses	Skills
Alternatives	Former employees	Learning by doing	Formal credentials
	Future employees	Reading an article	Unneeded skills
	Employees of other companies	Magically acquiring a skill	

Here we just selected "former employees" and pretended that they had "magically acquired the skills" rather than actually receiving training. And then we would interview them to understand their opinion.

Another scenario could be:

Components	Employees	Training courses	Skills
Alternatives	Former employees	Learning by doing	Formal credentials
	Future employees	Reading an article	Unneeded skills
	Employees of other companies	Magically acquiring a skill	

Why would we give a current employee an article about a skill that the company is not even interested in? Here's the reason why: there could be two major possibilities. One: they suggest that the article was useless, or two: on the contrary, they say they liked it. If we begin to see a pattern that employees are interested in acquiring skills that the organization clearly does not need, might it be a possible hint that they are not interested in building a career at this company? Maybe or maybe not, but it would certainly warrant further discovery.

Some fascinating examples of indirect probing come from the wisdom of previous generations. This Eastern European fairytale is a good specimen of probing in a complex environment. The task of the fairytale plot is to teach a young man the value of money:

There was a man who had a lazy son who never earned any of his own money. The father was healthy and strong and was able to feed and take care of the family, but as he got older he began to worry about his son. He said to his wife, "I think I should give all my estate to somebody else because my son doesn't know the value of money and will just squander it all."

His wife said, "I think you are wrong about him; he's a good boy."

The father replied, "If you really believe so, let him go and get a job, and when he earns his pay, let him bring it to me, so I can see it. If he does this, then I will let him inherit our estate."

The mother went to the son, gave him some money and said: "Go spend the day somewhere and come back in the evening. Then give your father this money and tell him you have earned it."

The boy did exactly that and when he handed the money to his father in the evening, the boy said, "Here. I earned this, just like you said I should."

The father took the money, stared at it for a while, and then threw it in the stove and watched it burn up. He said, "I don't think you earned this money, son."

The young man said nothing to his father, but his mother became even more worried. The next morning she gave him money again, and said, "Take this and go, but before you come back in the evening, run around a little so you become sweaty, and your father will believe you earned it this time."

And so he did, coming back wet with sweat, and handed the money to his father.

The father looked at the money again and threw it in the stove, just like before, and said, "I don't think you earned this, son."

The son shrugged and went back to his mother again. The mother finally realized she had taught her son the wrong lesson and said: "We were wrong in trying to fool your father. Go and find yourself a job, and whatever they pay you, bring the money to your father."

The young man listened to his mother, woke up early the next morning, and found himself some work for the day. He worked hard until sunset, collected his wages, and was so tired he could barely crawl back home. The father stared at the money and threw it in the stove, as before.

This time, however, the young man leaped across the room to the stove and began to pull the money out of the hot flames. "What have you done, father? I broke my back all day for this, and you just threw it in the fire!"

"Now," said the father, "I believe you really earned it. When you earn something, you know the true value of it."

In the fairytale, the father's actions revealed the missing information and led him to the correct conclusion about his son, but it was not a direct, or obvious way of probing. It was a creative approach, another way of looking at the problem, and a good example of how indirect probing might provide vital information about the complex system by looking at it from a new angle.

The Cost of Treating Complex Tasks as Simple

The human mind has many propensities, and two have a deep impact on the way we deal with tasks.

The first one has to do with how we perceive reality around us. We may think we see the world the way it actually is, but this is not true. Our perceptions of the things around us are not neutral or objective but conditioned by our motivations. This vital biological mechanism allows us to focus on what matters most to our survival at the very unconscious level. At any given moment, our explicit goals or implicit needs influence what we pay attention to. On a table you have an apple, a set of car keys and today's mail:

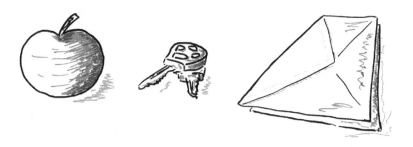

Map 4-5

But your brain rarely treats the objects on the table as they appear here. If you run by the table when you're really hungry, you will actually see something like this:

89

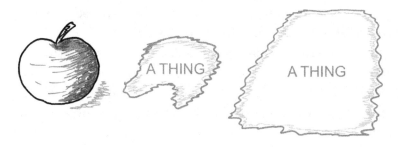

Map 4-6

This isn't something you *choose* to see. The "choice" is being made by the deepest circuits in your brain, changing the way your perception works. If you passed by the table when you were late for work, you might see this:

Map 4-7

When you're not hungry and not on your way out, perhaps you would see this:

Map 4-8

The second propensity determines how perception translates into a meaningful mental model of reality. When dealing with a new situation, the brain seeks to create a coherent story to describe the situation and tends to automatically fill all perception gaps with answers. What matters to the brain is not how *accurate* the story is, but rather how *coherent* it is. We experience a state of cognitive ease when the brain finds a story coherent, and the mind is restless until it finds a coherent story. Our brain is wired to jump to conclusions that seem to "make sense". Jumping to conclusions is vital when the speed of response is more important than the accuracy of the mental model of reality. These basic survival situations have guided the natural selection of our species and helped shape our genome. Our ancestors would have been unlikely to survive if instead of running from a bear, they stopped for a minute to analyze the situation more deeply to determine if there is a chance that they are just being prejudiced against a poor animal who, despite its aggressive appearances, may actually have a mellow, pleasant personality, deep down inside. No, our predecessors survived precisely because their brains instantly analyzed the situation and immediately created a super-low-resolution model of reality: "bear... danger... run...". And that was good enough to pass their genes on to the next generation in our grand family tree. In fact, it's hard to overemphasize the value of this mechanism: it is due to your and my ancestors' ability to quickly jump to conclusions that I have the luxury to write about it and you have the opportunity to read it.

A lot of the tasks we deal with today, however, are the exact opposite of basic survival situations where you had to think fast and the speed of decision-making was more important than the accuracy. We often have plenty more time to think and the accuracy of a mental model of reality becomes paramount. But our brain essentially remains unchanged, historically wired for an entirely different routine: it is conditioned by needs and goals in terms of perception and routinely jumps to conclusions. In other words, our brain has a natural propensity, forged by countless cycles of evolution, to treat complex tasks as more simple. And that is why we must apply extra caution when operating in the enterprise environment. We need to be exceptionally self-aware and open-minded regarding the nature of the various tasks at hand. While there are many simpler organizational tasks, there are also many tasks that are inherently complex and we're rarely given a special warning about which is which.

It is impossible to know for certain whether a new task is inherently complex or rather simple, but there are some hints that you might be dealing with a complex task:

1 The desired outcome of the system is a new behavior of individuals or a group of people

2 The outcome depends on human judgment regarding a future reality that doesn't yet exist

3 The task involves a change in parameters linked to human motivation

In an enterprise environment, a "presumption of complexity" is a good way to combat our natural assumptions of simplicity. It's much better to learn a task was simpler than you thought than the other way around.

To protect against "simplicity bias", an organization must establish explicit mechanisms for dealing with unknown unknowns. It's that simple.

There is a high price to mismanaging unknown unknowns and being under-equipped to deal with complex tasks. Your organization may be executing a plan that will create complete or partial waste. If there is no viable mechanism for uncovering unknown unknowns, the problem remains hidden under a layer of positive assurances and great expectations, ready to deliver a deadly strike at a time when no one is expecting anything to go wrong.

Organizational Impediments to Managing Unknown Unknowns

Some organizational factors amplify the human tendencies toward selective perception and jumping to conclusions, which builds pathological underestimates of task complexity into the organizational culture and way of operating.

Effort bias

Effort bias manifests itself when an organization concerns itself with the effort associated with the task, but disregards the learning process required for successful task execution. Instead of seeing all three important components of a task (effort, known unknowns, and unknown unknowns), the organization only pays attention to the first, and because this way there's no differentiation between entirely trivial tasks and really complex ones, the results can be catastrophic.

Map 4-9

A milder form of this problem occurs when the organization acknowledges the need to manage known unknowns, but still lacks any effective approach to addressing the unknown ones. (This gets usually encouraged by speculative risk-management frameworks that many enterprises utilize. Getting risks flashed out in a spread-sheet creates an implicit, comforting belief that "these are *all* the risks" that can be faced, while in fact, these are precisely the *known* ones. And the more complex the task, the more impactful are the unknown risks.) This manifestation of effort bias, exacerbated by speculative risk management practices, has a strong potential to create serious trouble for the organization.

Effort bias is very common and a lot of organizations don't realize they are subjected to it. To make sure your organization doesn't fall into the same trap, pay close attention to the following aspects of complex initiatives in your organization:

- Plan of intent
- Progress measures
- Success indicators
- Task lifecycle management

What is in your "Plan of intent"? Does your plan describe what should be built/created/developed in order to succeed with the initiative? Of course, it does. But does it contain anything else of substance? If your plan doesn't have a specific, practical approach to uncovering unknown unknowns, you have a real problem. Ask similar questions about "Progress measures" and "Success indica-tors". What is normally reported as "progression"? The amount of work done? If you hear more about what is being done or com-pleted than what has been learned, it's a sign of effort bias. But if an organization incorporates learned lessons into the plan, succeeding with its complex initiatives is much more likely.

Lastly, "Task lifecycle management", deserves much attention. Task lifecycle management may include organizational guidance, home-grown "best practices" and some visual tooling (electronic or physical) for tracking task progress. The question is the same as before: what do you see? If what you see is mostly work-oriented, and has little if anything to do with managing unknowns, then there is again a problem. If you want to change the way your organization or team manages complex initiatives, the areas mentioned above (the plan of intent, progress and success measures, and life-cycle management) should begin reflecting the way in which you intend to manage unknowns; especially the unknown ones. You can't expect any real change in people's mindset and work habits if these four areas continue to reflect legacy thinking. There is one important point that the organization needs to embrace:

Complex tasks progress at the speed of managing unknowns. Doing the wrong work faster is false progress. For complex tasks, the ability to navigate is more important than velocity.

The sooner an organization understands that, the better.

Dysfunctional Hierarchies

In Chapter 2 we touched on organizational hierarchies and how they might amplify disconnects (see Map 2-1). A poor approach to managing unknowns is a form of disconnect, caused by the underlying factor that good news travels effortlessly, while bad news is filtered out. Plans already established and approved by the higher levels in the organization carry a strong expectation that everything is progressing properly, and any newly discovered unknown is a threat to that expectation. The lower levels in the hierarchy will think twice before letting any bad news spread further up the chain of command. To reverse this dynamic, leaders at different levels must resolutely manifest—by action rather than by articulation—that they will be receptive and appreciative to learn empirical facts from the front line, regardless of how those facts align with the original expectation.

Big Upfront Planning

Big upfront planning forces assumptions, creates problems for the complex initiative and also reinforces a dangerous culture of indulging confirmation bias on a grand scale. Big upfront planning, however, is very easy to defend, especially because leaders prefer certainty to uncertainty. But just because we like certainty, doesn't mean that we should bypass the discovery process. Due to delayed feedback, there are consequences to wholesale assumptions, usually bad ones. The planning horizon must be shortened to alleviate this problem.

Fragmented Organizational Structure

Imagine two simple scenarios:

1   Your task is fully contained within one organizational unit

2   Your task requires the collaboration of two units

Both scenarios might involve the same number of people, but in the first case, they are all together in the same group, whereas in the second case they are separated. Separation often creates impediments to progressing with the task: everything becomes slower, there are more surprises and more inconsistencies. With that in mind, any progress will be harder in scenario "2" compared to scenario "1". But separation also causes disadvantages in managing unknowns. In case "1", fewer people possess a holistic view of the task and only understand their own part clearly. The separation between groups leads to a disconnect from outcomes and a focus on outputs, as discussed in Chapter 3 and shown in Map 3-11.

Within an organization, different groups are often built around different areas of expertise, or specific functions, or can be components of a larger solution. It is much harder to coordinate the efforts of such groups, which causes a disconnect from the outcome of the initiative. The "easiest" way to manage a distributed group is by defining specific outputs for each, but this immediately creates a problem: a team given the goal of delivering a specific output, without understanding the outcome of the larger task, will never question if it is the right output, to begin with.

Artificial Complexity and How Known Things Magically Become Unknown

Tasks become harder to accomplish, as the scale becomes larger. While it is true that "scale adds complexity" in natural and inevitable ways, complexity can increase even without adding scale. In many cases, this is a kind of complexity that could be avoided – something we call *artificial complexity*. Here are a few examples of artificial complexity:

* Rob and Erik are working on a new marketing campaign. Rob is a content editor and Erik is a graphic designer. They've worked together successfully many times before. They understand how important collaboration is for their work, and have habitually included lots of screen sharing, live conversations, editing shared notes, and so on, in the past. But the company started a process transformation with departments going through training and workshops led by a consulting company. Each unit had to establish a strong routine of planning and executing work and that essentially required people in a unit to spend significantly more time with their peers in the same unit. Rob and Erik were in different departments and had to devote more time and energy to their own groups. Shortly after this change, Rob and Erik began to discover unpleasant surprises in their work that had never occurred before. This increase in unknowns is easy to explain. Using the old process, any uncertainty about how to proceed would be resolved on the spot with a quick discussion on a shared electronic whiteboard or even a quick test of an idea on a computer with a shared screen. When Erik was in doubt about whether to use a single-column or double-column

layout for the brochure text, he would quickly show Rob what each layout would look like, and Rob could help decide which one was better for the text copy he was working on. But once Erik had to be more active within his own unit, this instant interaction was no longer an option. Instead of quickly figuring out which option is better, Erik now has to make an assumption and continue on, and Rob has to make assumptions of his own. As more assumptions are made, significant rework is required. These delays could have been avoided if Rob and Erik weren't arbitrarily and artificially separated from each other.

- The leadership of a software development team decided to introduce metrics that would allow them to measure the team's productivity. One of the metrics was the average lead time for the team's work items, and the importance of *improving* the lead time was made clear. The team decided to improve lead time at any cost, and naturally, the easiest path to improvement was by eliminating steps causing the most delays. Customer testing often caused delays, due to coordination difficulties, but cutting corners in customer testing caused a spike in production issues because the team had artificially introduced new unknowns by making false assumptions.

- A team gets a new leader who is obsessed with micromanaging the specific ways the team goes about performing their tasks. Because virtually all decisions are made by their boss, team members no longer pay attention to the nature of those decisions. After a while, this causes the quality and efficacy of the team's deliverables to decrease significantly. Things the team would have easily previously spotted due to their direct exposure to the context of work, have now become unknown to the actual decision-maker. These additional unknowns are artificially created as a side product of the new style of leadership.

- To improve the productivity of IT support, an organization decides to eliminate the existing support model, where internal customers contact a specific person on the support team, who over time learned more about their customer context and seemed to be able to provide decent service. The new model, however, ignored any prior customer relationship and sought to enhance response times by having a more elastic capacity allocation in a larger pool of IT support professionals. Due to the complexity of the IT system, randomly assigned people were unaware of all potential consequences of their actions, and so unexpected issues appeared in different corners of the organization. All the context-specific knowledge that had emerged over the course of months and in some cases even years, was canceled by this change, and things that had been known began morphing into unknowns.

- A group decides to introduce more rigor to the financial accounting of their initiatives, and so a specific, detailed cost-benefit breakdown must be provided before approval is given. Even though this is often just "creative writing", the teams are bound to follow the plan that has been outlined in the cost-benefit analysis. Much of this upfront analysis is essentially speculation, and naturally, a lot of the speculation proves to be wrong. But people assume that once a plan has been approved it must be followed, so the discovery occurs too late in the process. The speculations resulting from the approval process are artificially introduced unknowns.

Knowns can become unknowns all too easily. Something that was a known fact might no longer reach the people who need to know it, because of artificially created disconnects. As a result, such a "fact" may end up being a big surprise to some in the organization. Similarly, something may have been a known unknown, but due to an introduced disconnect, becomes an unknown unknown.

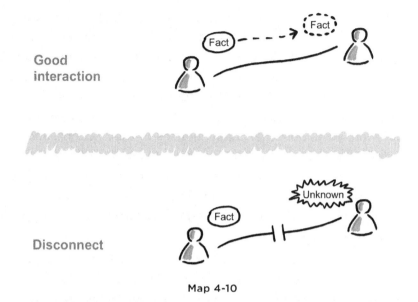

Good
interaction

Disconnect

Map 4-10

Notice that in all five of the previous examples, there was a good intention behind the change. But as the old saying goes: the road to hell is paved with good intentions.

To address artificial complexity, it is important to know what it is you are addressing. The mechanisms for discovering artificial complexity are the same as we described in Chapter 2 because at its core, artificial complexity is caused by some form of disconnect.

Some of the disconnects underlying artificial complexity might not be so easy to resolve. The best course of action is usually to address the *underlying causes*, to eliminate the extra complexity. Sometimes artificial complexity has to be accepted and dealt with as is. It boils down to managing unknowns by probing. A point of caution: yes, complexity can be dealt with by probing, but this should not become an organization's excuse for introducing unnecessary complexity. Artificial complexity can pile up very quickly and comes with a serious penalty.

The Fuzzy Boundary Between Known and Unknown Unknowns

To understand why the line between known and unknown unknowns is blurry, we need to add some structure to our concept of unknowns. The most basic anatomy of an unknown could be pictured as follows:

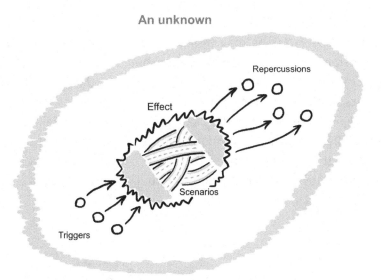

Map 4-11

The effect is the essence of the unknown, and what we care about the most in an unknown. It usually derives directly from the description of the unknown. If we had an unknown of "decreased employee satisfaction", then the effect is exactly that: "decreased employee satisfaction". Triggers are conditions or behaviors of the system that produce an effect. A potential trigger for decreased employee satisfaction could be new leadership that fails to connect with employees. Repercussions are what follows if the effect takes place. Repercussions of decreased employee satisfaction could be higher attrition and poor company image in the job market. Lastly, an effect can manifest itself in a broad variety of scenarios.

Decreased employee satisfaction may manifest through dissatisfaction with compensation, career progression, learning opportunities, and so on. Generally speaking, triggers, scenarios, and repercussions are intimately connected with each other. Some triggers may lead to specific scenarios, which lead to specific repercussions.

Imagine that you suspected a potential danger that your new accounting software could encounter issues with external data feeds. "Problem with external feeds" is a *known* unknown because you know what to look for, but the triggers, the actual scenarios, and the repercussions may be completely beyond current comprehension. There are many reasons that triggers could be hard to account for. Data feed failure can be triggered by incompatible formats, data duplicates, and many other variables. If the triggers are not understood, then the likelihood of the effect taking place is basically unknown. If repercussions are not well understood then the impact is hard to assess. So, even though we consider it a known unknown, not very much is actually known about it.

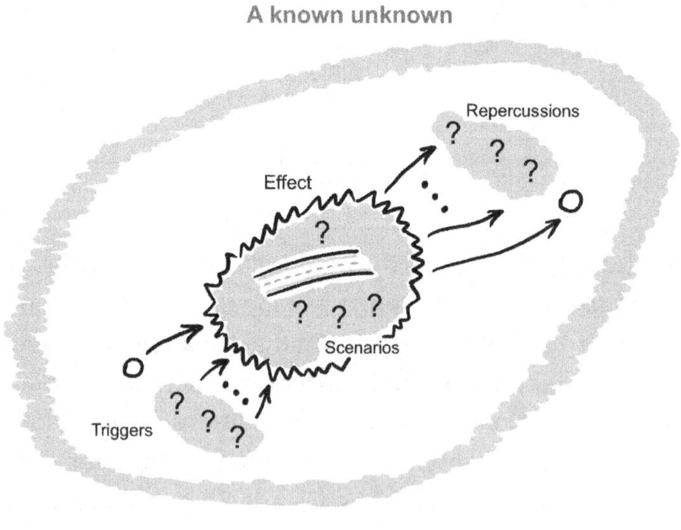

A known unknown

Map 4-12

Something labeled as a known unknown may easily create a false sense of security and lead to a specific problem:

A known unknown may contain unknown unknowns as its constituent parts. Triggers, scenarios, or repercussions of a known unknown may themselves be unknown unknowns and thus require respective probing techniques.

Probing in a Complex Outcome Chain

In complex outcome chains consisting of both immediate and higher-order outcomes, unknowns may appear at any level. Probing only for immediate outcomes can be dangerous because it may lead the task force towards the wrong ultimate objective. As we saw in Chapter 3, a disconnect anywhere in a complex outcome chain jeopardizes the ultimate outcome, and therefore outcomes at all levels should be carefully examined.

The higher the order of the outcome, the harder it is to probe for, and generally slower and costlier to probe for, so different probing approaches, and perhaps a different frequency of probing, should be applied at different nodes on the outcome chain.

Let's illustrate this using an example from Chapter 3 with the following outcome chain:

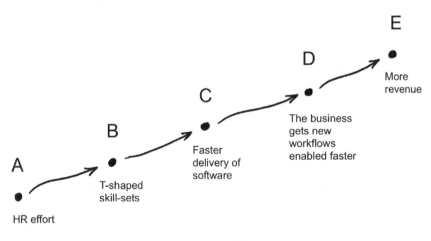

Map 4-13

The task is to create more business value by fostering the T-shaping process of employee skill-sets. If we wanted to utilize direct probing, it would be really hard to do as a single sweep across the whole chain. It is a lot easier to probe at node "B", and this can be done repeatedly by picking different subsets of employees and skills to see whether the new skills are being successfully acquired by the T-shaping method. Here we need to keep an eye open for any other discoveries along the way because it's an opportunity to unravel some possible unknown unknowns. At some point, we'd like to see if those skills really make the delivery of new software features faster, so we need to probe at node "C". It may be that the skills acquired as a result of T-shaping are too superficial to be useful outright. Or maybe we miscalculated the bottlenecked skill-sets, and the newly planned software shifts the demand towards a different set of skills we have not yet anticipated.

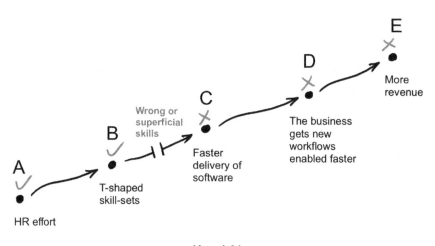

Map 4-14

Or maybe something completely different is discovered as a result of probing at node "C".

It may be tempting to assume that probing at nodes "B" and "C" would reveal most of the important gaps, but the process needs to be continued through the entire chain. By making too many assumptions when managing complex effort, crucial unknown unknowns will be overlooked. Probing node "D" may reveal that T-shaping resulted in expanding skill-sets, and sped up software development, but then the groups used their new skills to work on things relevant to those skills rather than what was most important to the users, leading to failure at node "D".

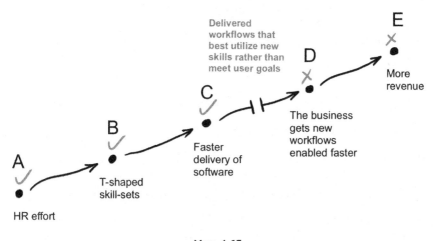

Delivered workflows that best utilize new skills rather than meet user goals

More revenue

The business gets new workflows enabled faster

Faster delivery of software

T-shaped skill-sets

HR effort

Map 4-15

The situation at node "E" might be very similar, with the functionality delivered by the group being satisfactory for the user, but that functionality not generating increased revenue.

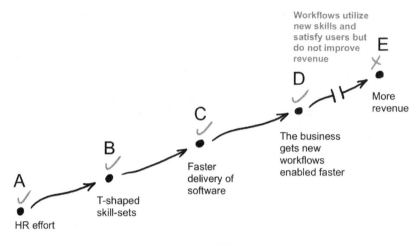

Map 4-16

Probing in complex chains may end up giving even more peculiar results. As we mentioned in Chapter 3, outcomes of complex tasks are often emergent in nature and may evolve in unexpected directions. To determine whether this is good or bad news we need to examine how this alternative outcome would impact higher-order outcomes in the chain. If the group has failed to T-shape, perhaps they discovered during their attempt that some of the modules of the software system could be easily rewritten in a different technology, with a skill-set that is not bottlenecked.

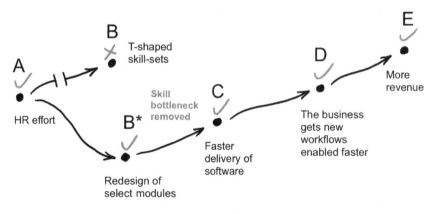

Map 4-17

Those modules might have accumulated a significant degree of technical debt and would have benefited from either a redesign or a rewrite, as a collateral benefit. The solution that emerged has nothing to do with T-shaping, yet it effectively enables higher-order outcomes, and that's what was needed.

Probing only for lower-order outcomes in a complex outcome chain may inhibit critical discoveries, so let's consider some probing strategies which work effectively across the entire chain:

1   Utilize more frequent incremental probing for the lower-order outcomes and less frequent probing for higher-order ones

2   Compensate with non-incremental probing for higher-level outcomes

In other words, the "volume" of incremental and non-incremental probing can be spread across the outcome chain like this:

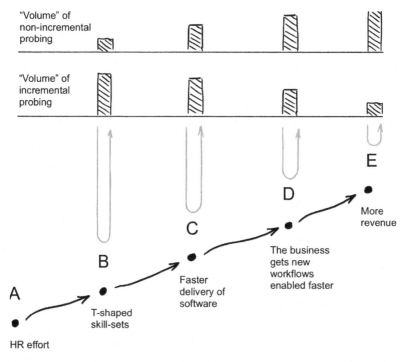

Map 4-18

Other helpful strategies may involve more of the indirect probing for higher-order outcomes to compensate for lack of fast and effective incremental probing at the higher level.

Analysis vs. Probing

Action, rather than speculation, is so important in probing because complex tasks cannot be fundamentally figured out. Complex systems can be "provoked" to reveal some of their internal mechanisms, which might give enough information to adjust the course of action and take the next step. And that's why obsessing with speculation is detrimental to the task's outcome: the mind can go down a long and exciting path, perhaps calling it a "plan", that might have nothing to do with reality. Without relentless probing for empirical evidence, you could be the last one to know about the task's failure.

With that caution in mind, however, speculation coupled with proper probing techniques can have merit, under the condition that there is a way to neutralize or significantly mitigate confirmation bias. Confirmation bias is favoring facts that confirm the desired assumption and dismissing evidence that invalidates it. Organizations may unconsciously encourage it by their structure, policy, and process. In the subsection "The Cost of Treating Complex Tasks as Simple" earlier in this chapter, we considered the key cognitive propensities which reduce our ability to manage unknowns and underlie confirmation bias. We also learned that in many organizations these are amplified across ineffective hierarchies (see Map 2-1) and solidified with overly constraining planning and budgeting techniques. In some sense, organizations appear to be optimized to amplify confirmation bias, and very few of them counter it effectively.

There are two general strategies for mitigating confirmation bias, and we will consider some possible tactical approaches within each of them.

Strategy 1: Separation of Responsibilities

The idea behind this strategy is very simple: if person A has confirmation bias regarding a specific possibility A*, we will introduce person B with a competing bias toward possibility B*, so that the two biases cancel each other out. This old idea has had some success in the specific domain of quality assurance. A software developer is paid to create new software and, because of a confirmation bias favoring her creation, cannot properly test the correctness of the developed functionality. A test engineer, on the other hand, is tasked and paid to find problems with the software system. The confirmation bias of a developer (seeking to prove that the functionality is correct) is largely neutralized by the confirmation bias of the tester (who is seeking to prove that the software *does not* function correctly). Similarly, in Chapter 3 we mentioned that the important role of outcome owner is often missing in an enterprise setting. This role depends on *detachment* from the outputs so that the best course of action can be selected without getting too comfortable with any specific solution, but rather seeking to advance the outcome itself.

US military and intelligence services fight confirmation bias by separation of responsibilities by forming a so-called "red team" tasked to find vulnerabilities in a high-stake plan of action. It's a simple solution to a severe problem. Adding more rigor to your risk management process will not help you manage unknowns within your organizational environment, because it will still be subjected to the same biases and cultural deficiencies as everything else. If you are genuinely concerned about confirmation bias, create a red team, and task them with discovering vulnerabilities in your plan of action.

Another approach is to consider multiple plans of intent at the same time. This works best when different people stand behind different plans, resulting in a "competition" across the plans. Probing competing plans from different angles can be so useful in revealing unknown unknowns, because a direct probing for solution option

A, may also be an indirect probing for solution option B. Referring to the subsection "Probing for Unknown Unknowns" above, what "approximates" the solution in one case may well "substitute" it in the other.

Strategy 2: Shift of Perspective

Confirmation bias can sometimes be mitigated even without separating responsibilities across different people. A "test-first" approach in software development takes advantage of an interesting trick: our mind becomes attached to code we've written, so let's try not to have any code when we "test". Instead of developing the actual functionality, we are only creating a "dummy" code that has programming interfaces but doesn't contain any internal logic. There's little room for confirmation bias because there's virtually nothing to be attached to, as there's no real logic implemented yet. The developer instead comes up with different test scenarios that could invalidate the "dummy". Those test scenarios are often captured as an automated test script and will persist for as long as the code itself persists. Once the "dummy" and the tests are in place, the developer can program the underlying logic, transforming the "dummy" into meaningful functionality.

A *pre-mortem* (also known as *proactive hindsight*) is a similar approach for finding gaps in a plan of action for any complex task. A group of people involved in an initiative get together, each one with a sheet of paper and a pen. The facilitator then suggests a brief journey into the future, where their existing plan of intent has been executed and the outputs were created, but the outcomes were not achieved. The facilitator then asks each member to independently write down the reasons why they think this happened.

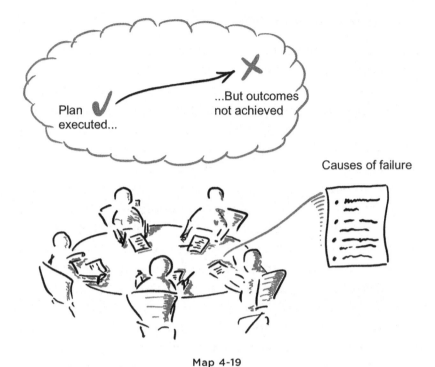

Map 4-19

After a few minutes of silent writing, each participant will read out their notes to the rest of the group. The group selects the key "causes of failure" from the read-outs, which might be used later to identify the missing enablers in the plan, or perhaps to revamp the plan entirely if a major flaw has been identified that invalidates the plan altogether.

Common Mistakes in Probing and How to Avoid Them

Here are some common mistakes made by organizations and teams that can lead to the ineffective management of unknowns.

Probing for Outputs Only

It is understandable to focus on tangible outputs as this provides a strong sense of security, which instills confidence. But that sense of security is false unless outcomes are probed for. Obsessing with outputs will lead an organization to burn up precious resources to produce inferior results. Familiar factors may be at the root cause of this obsession, including the funding and incentive model, established culture, leadership style, and so on. Initiating a conversation about outcomes can bring the leaders' attention to the actual repercussions of insufficient focus on outcomes. This conversation can be especially effective if based on real examples of poorly managed outcomes within the organization. These facts are usually accessible, just waiting to be used to improve the enterprise.

The next logical step is to try to diagnose what forces underlie inattention to outcomes. The list of common forces from Chapter 3 may help, but they do not always reveal the whole problem, and because complex environments can be quite diverse, it is dangerous to rely on a fixed list of possible culprits. Open-minded discovery is often worthwhile. Once you have selected a list of "suspects", it is important to remember that what you have is just a hypothesis, which requires validation. Probe fearlessly to prove it right or wrong or to learn something new about the problem.

Making Premature Conclusions

Many tasks have outcomes that emerge gradually over time, but the organization might hold on to an expectation that the outcome will follow quickly after delivering the outputs. It is a very dangerous conclusion, as it is common for complex environments to give an impression of moving in the desired direction at first, but then adjusting to the change and ending up absorbing most of the initial disruption. This can easily result in significantly reducing the desired effect, or even reversing the dynamic and producing negative repercussions. The "Black Diamond" example from Chapter 3 is a good illustration of this. One way to effectively probe in cases where the outcome is delayed in time is to make sure a sufficient amount of time has been given for a probe, so all the consequences of the probing action can thoroughly unfold, allowing the organization to see the actual outcomes. Alternatively, some sophisticated probing techniques can be used to achieve a faster turnaround time. When outcome emerges over a long period of time (due to the fact that various circumstances that impact the outcome, manifest gradually), more effective probing could be "speeding things up" and selecting for undesired circumstances early on to see how it affects the results. Various combinations of direct and indirect probing may help accelerate the process.

An outcome may emerge gradually when it depends on:

- Development of a habit
- Establishment of a social interaction
- Human learning process
- Change of mindset/culture

If the outcome does not involve any of the above, it doesn't imply you should make conclusions based on "fast" probing. Complex environments are fraught with surprises, and what may seem trivial at first, may actually involve unexpected mechanisms leading to delayed unanticipated effects.

Poor Approximation

It may be quite a challenge to approximate the desired state of the system well enough to draw conclusions from the probe. It might be difficult to get a proper approximation, but the organization may also overestimate the degree their experiment approximates the desired future reality. Sometimes a subtle detail plays a decisive role in this. This often happens, for example, when demonstrating a new increment of software to a user. The user may like it, but two months later, after actual deployment to production, the same user suddenly finds the software unusable. What was missing? What did we not approximate? Did we give the user insufficient exposure to the software system? Or did we fail to load meaningful data into the database so they could operate with something real? As all of that was provided in full, the missing detail turned out to be the actual *need* for using the software. When the user is really pressed to create their quarterly reports using this application, they will pay attention to things that didn't matter at all during the demo. The actual need to use a product is a very powerful force that is easy to overlook. Other complex tasks may involve crucial subtleties of a different kind, but this example underscores the challenge of selecting key factors to approximate.

Interpretation of Probing Results

So far we have talked a lot about probing as an experiment that renders valuable information. But we have made an implicit assumption: once the probing is done, the information—if useful—can be leveraged to correct the course of action and improve the task outcomes. That, however, is not the full story. The information that emerges from probing requires interpretation. And properly interpreting it, as it turns out, is not a trivial job at all.

Here are some examples that illustrate the levels of complexity associated with interpreting the results of probing.

An earlier example of indirect probing had employees read an article on an unneeded skill and then we asked for their opinions. We concluded that if employees demonstrated interest in the skill, then it *could* serve as evidence that they were not interested in advancing their careers with the organization. While there is some merit to this thought process, there are other potential explanations too. One of them might be just natural curiosity. Yet another is that people may want to advance their career at the current place of employment, but are tired of outdated work practices, and instead just seek to transition to better ways of working.

Another example relates to developing new human behaviors. A company is adopting a new enterprise accounting standard. The immediate desired outcome would be that the company's accountants are following the new standard. The standard is communicated to a subset of accountants, and the company immediately sees that those accountants seem to understand both the need for the new standard and how to use it in practice. But as tempting as it may be to call this probing successful, it may actually turn out to be quite the opposite. For starters, the accountants may be too optimistic early on with respect to the new practices, but being good corporate citizens, they decide to play along. That may easily change, however, as soon as the novelty of the practices wears off and old habits begin to seep through. And there's another reason why the initial interpretation may be wrong: it is one thing to ask someone's opinion regarding the new accounting practices; it is quite another thing, however, to use them when the time comes to prepare quarterly reports, etc. It may, in fact, turn out that the new standards are unusable, even though the initial information about it was very encouraging. This example is one of many where early probing results may be non-representative of the actual outcome. And in fact, they are non-representative because the probe provides a poor approximation of the future state of the system. But the real problem is that the organization may not even suspect that to be the case.

Probing in complex environments generally contains ambiguity, but especially when probing for unknown unknowns. Interpretation of any information is a process of reconciling that information with past experiences. But in complex environments, probing is supposed to provide *novel* information. And novelty always leads to ambiguity simply because it cannot be easily reduced to past experiences.

Where there is ambiguity, there's a danger that confirmation bias will hijack the results, because ambiguous aspects of the new information will likely be interpreted in a way that supports existing goals and expectations. If there is excessive speculation, at least an argument can be made that the system might not be figured out by an upfront analytical approach, and thus the speculative plan of action cannot be trusted. But if probing was done, the "excessive speculation" argument can no longer be made. In fact, it will be a lot harder to convince the organization that their plan of action is wrong because now it is "backed" by probing results. The biased interpretation destroys the value of probing and possibly puts the organization in the same position, in terms of knowledge, as if there had been no probing at all. Serious precautions should be taken.

To mitigate the impact of confirmation bias on the interpretation of probing results, some type of "red team", considered earlier, can be used to provide alternative interpretations. Also, a specialized pre-mortem can be held to find flaws in the existing interpretation. (In this case, a thought experiment would be to imagine that a particular interpretation was followed, but it turned out to be wrong. The participants would then list potential reasons the outcome was not achieved.)

Often an important step in finding viable interpretations is to make the interpretation process more explicit. Interpretations routinely happen no matter what, and when they are performed by the organization subconsciously, it makes confirmation bias much more likely to influence the results. But when interpretation is given importance and value, its chances of being treated more responsibly improve.

Interpretation should not be thought of as a single, perfectly unified, and aligned organizational process. Indeed, such a process would suggest a problem in the interpretation. In complex large-scale environments, genuine interpretations of discoveries are inherently diverse. Any time they become near-perfectly aligned, it is very likely that the opinions are being swayed in one way or another by some strong factor, either as a result of a conscious process (e.g. intentional pressure created by some leaders) or an unconscious one (e.g. due to a conformist culture). Whatever the cause, the effect denies the organization the vital ability to work out what's really going on. A good antidote against misinterpretation is to involve different people, from different levels and groups, in the interpretation process. Of course, this only works if the leadership seeks to enable the psychological safety of their employees, rather than simply assuming people feel safe in expressing honest opinions, so that information can meaningfully translate into progress on a complex task.

👥 Taking Action

1 Determine direct probing scenarios you would use to uncover unknowns for your complex task. To facilitate this:

    a Define key enablers of your task

    b Define approximations for each enabler

    c Consolidate them in a table and select different probing scenarios

2 Define one or two indirect probing scenarios. Consider using the substitution method to get started.

3 In both cases, make sure that you are probing for outcomes and not just for outputs. Apply techniques from Chapter 3 to refine your understanding of the task's outcomes.

4 Use pre-mortem to analytically explore gaps in your understanding of the task. Consider combining pre-mortem and probing (utilize pre-mortem as a way to identify areas that need probing).

5 Perform items 1-4 of this list not only on immediate but also on higher-order outcomes in your outcome chain.

CHAPTER 5

The Mystery of Business Value

Questions That Puzzle Every Enterprise

What's the business value of a partnership? Of a new marketing professional who joins the team? Of sales training? What is the business value of a new product or service the enterprise is working to deliver? Or a corporate email system? Or a new software feature? How about a business intelligence report highlighting the details of a company's operations? What is the business value of a process improvement?

Organizations need answers to questions like these because every business wants to create some form of value. Knowing how an asset contributes to this value is a basic need. It would be unusual for a company to never wonder how much value they are getting out of their investments.

But despite the great interest, organizations seldom get proper answers. Our goal will be to offer some tools to help find them. But this will not be an easy journey. No single answer will apply in all possible cases. The question of business value is too complex for such a universal mechanism to exist. Instead, we will have to peel away at the problem, layer by layer, at every step revealing the next level of vital intricacies of the question. We begin with simpler cases and provide answers sufficient to that level of complexity, and then gradually advance towards more complex examples.

With that in mind, let's get started with some key notions.

An Asset and Its Business Value

Above, we wondered about the business value of training, a person on the team, a product or service, a software feature, an email system, a report, and a process improvement. We refer to these as *assets*. An asset is anything that has the potential to generate business value for an organization, in any form. (Note that we use the term asset quite loosely and in a much broader sense than it is defined in accounting standards, for example.) Assets are extremely diverse: from very specific, tangible things, like a software system used for planning and tracking product logistics, to completely intangible ones, like the motivation of employees delivering a complex service.

We define business value as the *utility* that the asset provides to the organization. A successful process improvement allows faster and cheaper operations, and so this is the business value, or utility, of the improvement. A newly-hired marketing specialist can create a marketing campaign the organization needs to reach a broader customer base, and that is the business value in hiring that person. A corporate email system allows fast communication and document exchange – that's the business value it provides. These examples offer a good general idea, but further in this chapter, we will touch on more specific ways of expressing business value.

If we were able to determine the business value of an asset, how would we use it? Here are the key reasons why it is important to know business value:

- Effective funding. There are always limited resources available for investing in various assets, so choices must be made about what should and shouldn't be funded, how investments are funded, and how investments are prioritized at different levels of an enterprise.

- Opportunity to add more value. A higher value might be generated by using an asset more meticulously. This, however, is a particularly delicate topic and requires very careful treatment. Driving higher value from existing assets is too often attempted in a way that ultimately leads to more harm than benefit.

- Finding alternative solutions. Sometimes an asset is not the best solution to a problem and can be replaced by a better option, but this is a more complicated conversation that may require a more advanced strategy than simply replacing one asset with another.

These questions may arise at any level of an organization, high or low: from deciding whether to fund a billion-dollar infrastructure project, to choosing between two software features that could each be implemented by a small team of developers within a couple of weeks.

Introducing Value Paths

Doug is the CEO of a company that recently signed a partnership agreement with an organization (Company A) specializing in product distribution. Doug and his Board of Directors are curious to know if the partnership will match expectations, and Doug is eager to quantify the actual business value of the partnership.

Six months after signing the deal, the additional distribution channels made available through Company A have boosted Doug's revenue by 8%. The way Doug thinks about the value of a long-term partnership is by how much additional revenue it produces over the course of five years, which is the average timeframe he would expect a partnership deal to last. Based on the increase in the first six months, Doug extrapolates the total revenue increase over five years to be $30 million. This figure is an approximate expression of the business value of the partnership with Company A.

The partnership with Company A represents a relatively simple example of an asset because there is only a single way in which partnership with Company A benefits Doug's business: Company A creates additional sales revenue for Doug by utilizing their existing distribution channels.

Revenue
increase

$30 M

Partnership w/
Company A

Map 5-1

We will be calling the connector on the diagram a *value path,* or just *path.* This asset example is pretty straightforward because its value path diagram contains only a single path, and in this case, the business value is easily expressed in financial terms.

Doug's company signs another partnership agreement with Company B which will provide a distribution channel for Doug's product, as does Company A, but will also be a part of the manufacturing process by producing some physical parts for the product at a cheaper unit price than the existing vendor. When Doug sees the first quarterly report showing a 5% revenue increase and a 15% decrease in the cost of supplied parts, he makes a five-year projection that looks as follows:

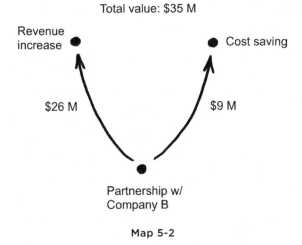

Map 5-2

The partnership with Company B is slightly more complicated because it has two value paths, one leading to revenue increase and the other to cost saving. As both outcomes can be expressed in financial terms, it is easy to see the total business value of this partnership.

Company B is a more valuable partner than Company A, producing $5 million more in business value, and if Doug's company wanted to focus on one partner only, it would make sense to choose to continue working with Company B.

In case when an asset's impact on the outcome is directly measurable in financial terms, the value discovery process is:

1 *Identify all value paths from the asset to outcomes*

2 *Define value score for each path in financial terms (V1, V2 , ...)*

3 *Add the values of all paths to get the total asset value (V1 + V2 + ...)*

Let's look at a different organization and use value paths to try to determine the business value that a new marketing professional brings to the team.

We would like to be able to express business value in financial terms, but any ultimate revenue increase can hardly be traced back to the new team member's actions. Instead, there will be a few intermittent outcomes on the outcome chain:

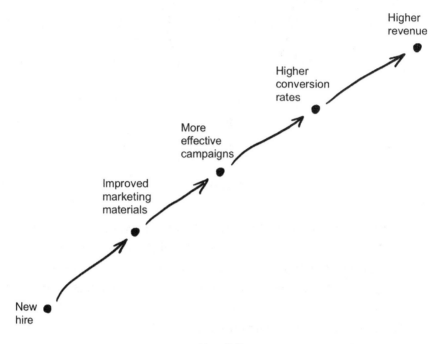

Map 5-3

The new hire could contribute to the immediate outcome in different ways, but it is difficult to say how revenue will be influenced in the end because so many other factors are also contributing to the ultimate outcome. A different approach is needed.

Instead of speculating about a revenue increase that would result from a new hire, we will tap into the outcome chain at a much lower level—at the level of the immediate outcome—"Improved marketing materials". We do this because this way we can have a reasonable conversation about how to best enable this (immediate) outcome and what type of person would be a good fit, so we could make a more effective hiring decision. In other words, we substitute the question "What's the impact of a new marketing hire on revenue?" with "What's the impact of a new marketing hire on the ability to create marketing campaigns?" Such a substitution must always be used with caution: optimizing for immediate outcomes without validating assumptions further down the outcome chain can be dangerous. But with that caution in mind, let's continue.

In order to produce the desired marketing materials, a person has to be able to create a good marketing text copy, design basic layouts in a graphic design tool, and optimize the content for search engines and social media. This can be described in the following value path map:

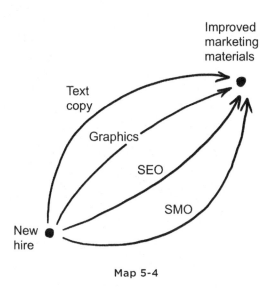

Map 5-4

Our theory is that if these four aspects are properly taken care of, it should lead to more effective campaigns. Let's assume that a more effective campaign results in a higher number of customer conversions. What differentiates this example from the case with Doug's company is that for Doug's company, each path was adding value independently. In this example, however, each path contributes to the overall value but cannot deliver it independently. A campaign cannot be created simply as a text copy or only as a graphic material. All four aspects are required: text copy, graphics, SEO, and social media optimization. This means that no single path can be measured in isolation or evaluated independently. We can only determine how much each path *contributes* to the outcome, relative to one another. Because we don't actually need units of measure here, we can express the relative "importance" of each value path as percentages, or just as a number with no unit of measure. We could define the importance of different skills of a marketing specialist in creating good marketing materials for this particular company as:

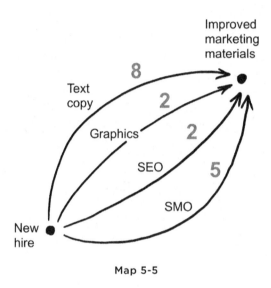

Map 5-5

This tells us that the ability to create good text copy is roughly four times more important than the graphics, and that ability to optimize content for the use in social media is about 2.5 times more important than the search engine optimization, for this type of campaigns.

Using simple integers is often a very convenient and practical method, and can easily be transformed into percentages simply by dividing each integer by the sum of scores across all paths and multiplying by 100:

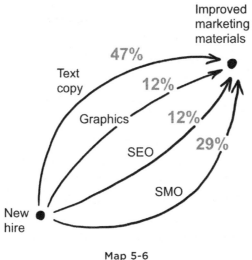

Map 5-6

We will see an important application of percentages later in the chapter but for now let's stick to integer scores, like in Map 5-5.

The set of integer numbers can be used as simple criteria to select good candidates for the job. All we need to do is assess each of the four skills for each candidate during the interview. After interviewing three candidates for the job, the interviewers might end up with the following table:

Candidate	Text copy skill level (Skill$_1$)	Graphics skill level (Skill$_2$)	SEO skill level (Skill$_3$)	SMO skill level (Skill$_4$)
Tanya	3	5	1	2
Andrew	5	1	3	1
Liz	7	1	1	1

Now we substitute those values into a simple formula for the total score, derived from our value path diagram (Map 5-5):

Candidate Score = $8 \cdot \text{Skill}_1 + 2 \cdot \text{Skill}_2 + 2 \cdot \text{Skill}_3 + 5 \cdot \text{Skill}_4$

The calculated results are:

Candidate	Skill$_1$	Skill$_2$	Skill$_3$	Skill$_4$	Calculation	Candidate Score
Tanya	3	5	1	2	8·3+2·5+2·1+5·2	46
Andrew	5	1	3	1	8·5+2·1+2·3+5·1	53
Liz	7	1	1	1	8·7+2·1+2·1+5·1	65

The table shows that the formula favors Liz, who is very proficient in the highest-valued skill for this job. We were able to assess this without resorting to any absolute numbers and used relative values instead. Additionally, departing for a moment from higher-order outcomes and focusing on the immediate ones, helped uncover a vital level of detail.

In case of a complex, multi-tiered outcome chain, the value discovery process can be performed as follows:

1 Identify the full outcome chain

2 Determine all value paths connecting the asset to immediate outcomes

3 Define the relative importance (I_1, I_2, ...) of each path to the outcome

4 Determine the asset capabilities score for each value path (C_1, C_2, ...)

5 Calculate the value score for each path ($V_1 = I_1C_1$, $V_2 = I_2C_2$, ...)

6 Calculate the overall value of the asset ($V_1 + V_2 + ...$)

This process is very similar to the one in Doug's example, but with some extra steps. We were able to directly determine the value score for each of Doug's partnerships because each path shared a unit of measure: the dollar. A dollar earned in sales revenue can be compared to a dollar saved by a more effective supply process. In the current case, however, we have different value paths corresponding to different asset capabilities that cannot be directly compared to one another. That is why we introduced the "importance" factors that allow us to "convert" different asset capabilities to a common notion of overall value. Think of importance factors as an "exchange rate" for different asset capabilities. If you have two amounts (X and Y) in two different foreign currencies, just adding the numbers makes no sense, but if each currency has an exchange rate to US dollars (A and B, respectively) then AX would be the value of the first amount in USD and BY is the value of the second amount in USD, making them comparable to one another. As a matter of fact, the overall value can now be calculated by adding AX and BY. In the same way, the importance factor "creating text copy" does not contribute to value the same way as "SEO", and so they require a "conversion".

Further in the chapter, we will consider some additional factors that may influence the accuracy of this approach. Even in our example with a marketing professional, there may appear complicating factors that would require a more advanced value assessment tool. In some high-stake situations, the use of more advanced tools can be justified and that is something we will explore later.

Please keep in mind that in making comparisons so far, we have assumed that all options came at the same cost and that the economic choice between the options would, therefore, depend only on the benefit. If the actual cost of the assets that are being compared is different, then the business value would have to be divided by cost prior to comparison. For the sake of simplicity, we will continue to make the assumption that the cost of compared assets is the same throughout the rest of this chapter.

How to Compare Apples to Oranges?

When competing for any limited resource, like funding, many of the questions that come up require us to compare assets that are not easily comparable.

Map 5-7

So far we have outlined a methodology for working with comparable assets, and the tools we've introduced help us make choices, whether between multiple candidates competing for the same job, multiple vendor applications considered to replace an existing enterprise app, or different security protocols to keep the organization safe. But oftentimes a different question needs to be answered. Instead of asking whether Tanya, Andrew, or Liz are the best hire for the marketing specialist position, the question is what should we rather do, hire more marketing specialists or use the money to push the existing campaigns down some conventional channels such as social media ads. Or rather than trying to figure out which accounting application to purchase, we would have to decide between purchasing an application vs. sending the accountants to a training. It might not be easy to answer such questions, and they cannot be answered by directly applying the approach we've used so far.

If we had some kind of common denominator, an expression for these assets in financial terms, all of these questions would be very easy to answer. But when an asset is at the bottom of the outcome chain, many levels apart from the ultimate economic benefit, using money to express its business value is not practically achievable, however tempting it may be.

But we already know how to find the right answer. We just need to expand the approach we've taken so far, to be applicable to situations like this. Earlier when comparing different job candidates to one another, we used their impact on the immediate outcome of producing improved marketing materials as an expression for value. Similarly, if we had to distinguish between different accounting apps, it would be done based on how they benefit the immediate outcome. So to solve our problem we need to find the lowest-order outcome on the outcome chain that is impacted by both of the assets we are comparing:

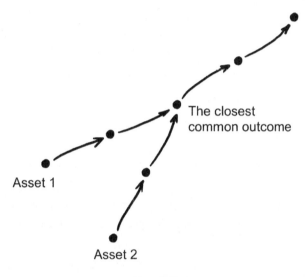

The closest common outcome

Asset 1

Asset 2

Map 5-8

In other words, we need to locate the *closest common outcome* (or outcomes) influenced by both assets, and then identify value paths, rank them, and finally aggregate the results to get the overall expression for value, just as we did before.

The "joint" outcome chain linking the choice between hiring marketing professionals and investing in new marketing channels, would be:

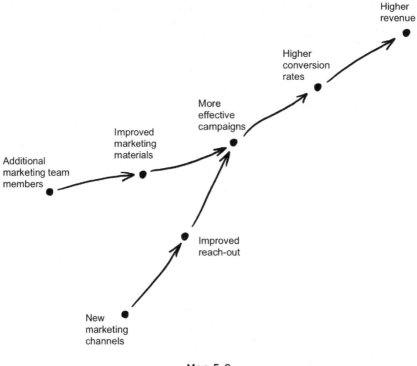

Map 5-9

The closest common outcome is "More effective campaigns". Now we need to define the key aspects of this outcome to use them as the key value paths so we can evaluate the two assets. We could say that "More effective campaigns" are campaigns with:

1 More relevant viewers

2 Stronger impact on a viewer

3 Social effect

4 Ability to outperform the competition

Just like before, each value path is going to be scored in terms of importance, relative to each other, like so:

1 More relevant viewers (3)

2 Stronger impact on a viewer (5)

3 Social effect (3)

4 Ability to outperform the competition (7)

The next step will be to score each asset's capability in enabling these value paths, and calculating the value across all paths:

Asset	Relevant viewers	Stronger effect	Social effect	Competitive	Calculation	Total Score
Additional marketing team members	3	5	7	2	3·3+5·5+3·7+7·2	69
New marketing channels	6	2	3	5	3·6+5·2+3·3+7·5	88

"New marketing channels" appears to be the most effective result in this case.

Similarly, if we needed to choose between updating the corporate accounting app and sending the accountants to training, we would have to find the closest common outcome on the outcome chain, which could be "Improved accounting team productivity", and use it to assess the two options by identifying the value paths and performing all the required scoring and aggregation.

And if we had to compare two software features and decide which one to develop and which one to postpone, we would use the same approach. The closest common outcome here would be satisfying the key user goals. The actual user goals would serve as the value paths to score each feature by.

In case of comparing two assets that perform different functions, the value discovery process will be:

1 *Find the closest common outcome to both assets on the outcome chain*

2   *Identify value paths that connect each asset to that outcome, and score the value paths by importance*

3   *Score capabilities of each of the two assets along the identified value paths*

4   *Calculate values for each path and aggregate the results*

Note that if comparing assets requires bypassing quite a few intermittent outcomes, the comparison will be, generally speaking, not very accurate. And conversely, the closer the common outcome is to the assets, the more accurate will be the calculation.

The Inherent Connection Between Business Value and Outcomes

Outcomes are crucial in determining business value. To find out what the business value of an asset was, we examined the impact the asset had on outcomes. Without understanding outcomes, business value has no meaning. When the landscape of desired outcomes changes, so does the business value.

But the connection also works in the opposite direction. Business value helps understand how well the outcome is realized. If more business value is achieved, we are happier with the outcome.

Outcomes provide meaning and structure to business value. Business value helps determine how effectively the outcomes are achieved.

Value Moderators

Even in examples that appear straightforward at first, not everything may be so simple. When Doug's company partnered with Company B, the initial projections turned out to be unsustainable beyond the first quarter. The quality of parts supplied by Company

B deteriorated causing Doug serious issues with customers, forcing him to switch his sourcing over to another vendor. The value path of partnership with Company B, instead of producing benefit, ended up creating overall damage, due to recalls and needing to switch over to a different supplier.

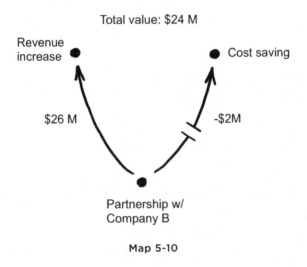

Map 5-10

This example is a good reminder that a value path may contain uncertainty: known and even unknown unknowns, making any situation more complicated than it appears.

To explore the uncertain behavior of value paths, let's consider the business value of sales training. It seems reasonable to think of a sales revenue increase as a desired outcome of the training because a team's ability to close more deals should generate more revenue. However, when the training was delivered by the same third party training provider to two different organizations, different outcomes were seen. Organization 1 received the training, but due to deeply ingrained fear culture, no salesperson changed their established ways of working which made the training practically useless. No sales revenue increase was detected.

Revenue
increase

Training in
Organization 1

Map 5-11

In Organization 2, open-minded leadership had long instilled the culture of curiosity, organizational learning, and courage to stride towards ambitious goals despite unknowns and hurdles along the way. The results even surprised the trainers. The salesforce started applying new techniques that streamlined better interaction with prospects and returning customers, but also made a few powerful and unexpected moves outside their conventional area of influence. First, they took the idea of customer empathy, learned in the training, a step further, and started acting as a strong source of input to the product development team, supplying them with important insights about the product that they routinely receive due to their direct exposure to the customer. The result was a series of product improvements that significantly broadened market reach within six months, simply from an increase in customer referrals. Second, because they were able to understand different customer personas, salespeople helped to complete the modeling of the customer journey, which enabled the marketing team to craft more effective campaigns. Finally, they also helped to make adjustments to the licensing model which improved revenue due to a higher level of flexibility. The detailed value path diagram for Organization 2 was:

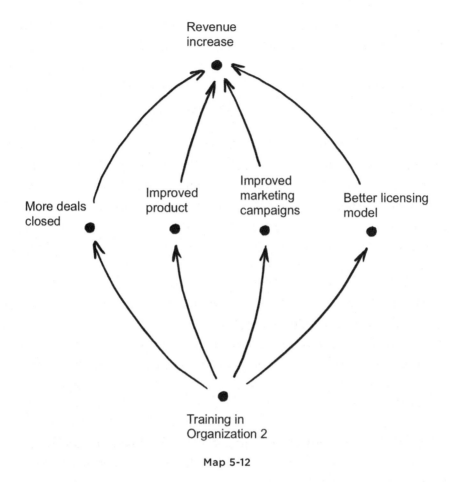

Map 5-12

The interesting thing about this value path map is that only the first path was intended, while the other paths were completely unexpected.

In complex cases, not only the actual value of a path may be not known upfront, but also novel value paths may emerge.

This is a good reminder that analysis is good, but it is a speculative tool and must be used alongside probing to achieve a sufficient level of confidence.

There are multiple reasons for caution about up-front speculative calculations. In the example of hiring a marketing specialist, it may be that the "importance" scores assessed for each value path were assessed incorrectly. Perhaps graphics design skill is actually far more important than we thought and so our candidate selection was suboptimal. This happens a lot, especially when dealing with skill estimation for new, not yet experienced, work. It's also possible that job interviews provided a positively or negatively skewed assessment of the candidates' skill levels. Inaccuracies can happen in both skill importance scores and skill levels scores. Treating both scores as subjects for additional validation could help reduce surprises. We must consider these possible inaccuracies as *known unknowns*. We could validate our assumptions, for example, by interviewing an existing employee who performs a similar job about how they would assess the importance of each skill, or someone could be asked to detail the tasks for the new job or even try to execute some of them. Such close contact with the problem could reveal a lot of valuable information.

Additional complexities may arise from a natural tendency to focus only on the most obvious skill required. But perhaps a more suitable person for the job would be able to establish good collaboration with the product development team, which portrays the product more effectively in the marketing campaign. This might actually be an example of a missing value path with a high importance score that would reveal itself only upon deeper exploration: an impactful *unknown unknown*.

Once again, probing is required to properly discover value paths. Probing should be used without hesitation and Chapter 4 provides a good toolset for that.

A mechanism called a *value moderator* is a tool that helps significantly with value discovery and streamlines both speculative analysis and probing for value. A value moderator is a factor that regulates how much value is actually being enabled by an asset. Value moderators are a kind of "reality check" to help guard against confirmation bias and wishful thinking. Some value moderators only affect one particular value path, while others might be able to act on multiple paths or perhaps even the entire ecosystem that contains the asset. We will depict a value moderator of a particular value path like this:

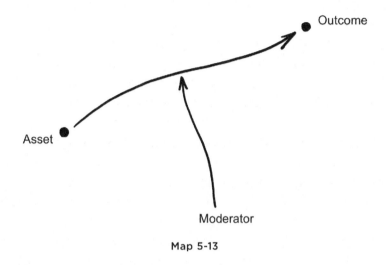

Map 5-13

We have already encountered value moderators in Doug's dealings with Company B, where the quality of supplied parts was a value moderator for the second value path:

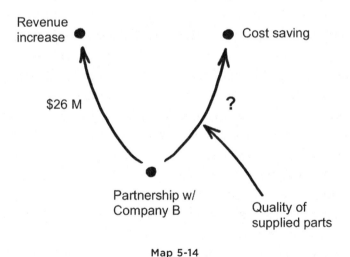

Map 5-14

This was actually a crucial moderator because when the quality of supplied parts went down it impeded value to such an extent that Doug abolished that entire value path and found another supplier.

Value moderators can provide both negative or positive effects on the outcome. In the sales training example, the culture of Organization 1 reduced value, and the culture of Organization 2 increased value, but we can say that organizational culture was a powerful value moderator in both companies.

Value moderators are particularly important when trying to assess and compare the business value of assets with different purposes. Multiple factors influence value yield because the closest common outcome is not usually the immediate outcome on the outcome chain. When we had to make a choice between hiring additional marketing team members or investing in new marketing channels, the score assigned to those assets was contingent upon quite a few assumptions and conditions. Were we considering hiring people with low or high experience levels? If we had hired low-experience people, would it be more beneficial to spend the money on a good advertising channel instead? If we had hired an extremely qualified team of marketing professionals, could they have been so creative with new campaigns that there would be higher differentiation from competitors, with higher impacts or more relevant viewers, and a higher social effect? That would likely tip the scales to the other side. In this case, the proficiency level of the marketing specialists hired is a very impactful moderator.

How do we discover value moderators? While some value moderators might be easily discovered, others may be hidden below layers of cognitive bias, only revealed by more sophisticated analysis tools such as pre-mortem (see Chapter 4). Oftentimes a mixture of methods is useful; sometimes analytical tools can reveal a value moderator, but the real impact of that moderator can only be discovered by probing. But a great deal of caution must be applied here because *emergent* value moderators cannot be discovered using speculative analytical tools. Deteriorating quality of parts was an emergent value moderator because some time after the partnership agreement was signed, someone at Company B got the idea to cut production cost by simplifying their manufacturing routines. The resulting poor quality was a side effect that was beyond what Doug's company could have reasonably envisioned.

Understanding value moderators is an important step in the value discovery process.

A value discovery process incorporating moderators is:

1 *Identify value paths connecting the asset to outcomes*

2 *Determine value moderators and their effects on value paths*

3 *Determine value scores of paths, taking into account the effects of moderators*

4 *Calculate values across all paths.*

Note that we have abbreviated some sections of the value discovery process for the sake of simplicity. For example, in Step 3 we assume that scoring importance and capability down each path have been used to get the path value score, just like it was done before.

Value moderators are a major component of finding ways to generate more value with an asset. Identify all significant moderators regulating a particular value path and see how they could be activated to boost the yield of the path. Some of them are costlier to activate, so prioritize which value moderators should be worked on.

Fractal Value Paths

Complex assets hide a trick: *composite paths*. A composite path is not actually a single path; instead, it has multiple subpaths underneath. A composite path is like a cable consisting of multiple little fibers underneath. Being able to write good marketing text copy has multiple components that may contribute differently to a particular task, involving proper writing style, grammar, storytelling, vocabulary, ability to connect with human emotions, and so on. But these subpaths are also split up into subpaths of their own. For instance, the ability to connect at a deep emotional level may split into subpaths that correspond to abilities to create a sense of urgency, empathy, empowerment, loyalty, curiosity, and so on. The skill of storytelling might be split into creating relatable characters, developing viable scenarios, and connecting to a customer's wants and needs.

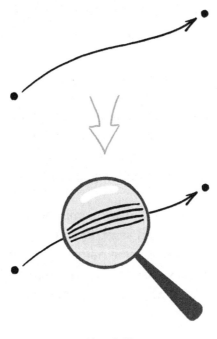

Map 5-15

Path structure matters because providing a wholesale assessment of a composite path may be quite dangerous. A subpath critical to the outcome might be pretty weak on the asset side in terms of capability while subpaths not important to the outcome might encompass quite a bit of capability on the asset side thus producing a mismatch.

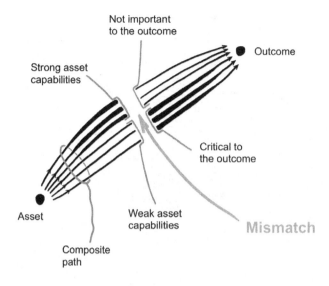

Map 5-16

For example, an interviewer may have concluded that a candidate has a good text copywriting skill but this was because the candidate showed great vocabulary, good grammar, and excellent overall writing style. At the same time, the candidate was not a good storyteller and could not connect well to human emotions, nor create some positive action bias that would ultimately translate into customer conversions. The candidate was never tested for these critical subpaths because the "text copy" part of the interview was just a free-form task to "write something", and the interviewer was supposed to assess it but with no structure reflecting what is important to the outcome. A more refined analysis is needed, especially when the cost of error is fairly high.

Some subpaths are themselves composite paths, and their constituent subpaths may be composite paths too, and so on, creating a sort of a fractal pattern. In this case, we call it a *fractal path*. If an asset has fractal value paths, we will call it a *complex asset*.

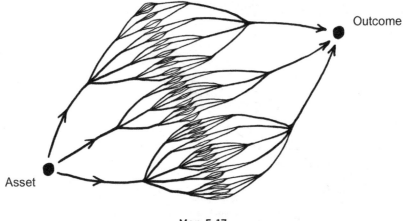

Map 5-17

A composite path is not necessarily fractal. A plain composite path that is just a collection of a few subpaths can be easily analyzed. A fractal value path, on the other hand, is a bottomless pit of ambiguity and uncertainty, as there's always another level, potentially hiding surprises. Two key questions are:

1   How do we know if an asset has fractal value paths?

2   How to identify the asset value if it has fractal value paths?

Let's try to answer the first question.

The marketing professional example is a representative of a pretty broad area of assets that have fractal value paths. This category is professionals with advanced skills or expertise. Not every skill, of course, falls in this category: there are simpler, repetitive functions that simply don't have a virtually unlimited number of small (but important) facets. But more and more enterprise tasks become complex and require advanced skill-sets. There are plenty of different domains besides marketing where a skill represents a fractal value path. An example of a pretty complex one would be software development. So, a skill of a server-side enterprise web application developer, for example, may split into the ability to program message queues, data validation rules, data structures, and so forth. The work with data structures, in turn, splits into the ability to work with collections and lists, custom data types, composition patterns, and so on. Working with collections is also composite in nature, consisting of the ability to create and utilize custom iterators, collection scan functions, aggregations over a collection, etc. And this may continue on and on, into deeper and deeper levels. And most importantly, depending on the work that needs to be performed, different subpaths may become critical to the outcome.

So, our first important category of assets is people and the fractal value paths are their advanced skills.

Another category of assets is complex software products. Whether vendor-based or homegrown, these are, by design, multi-faceted assets that are created to enable a broad multitude of value paths. A value path in this case, is, as you have probably already guessed, a user scenario. And those scenarios often split into sub-scenarios that split into sub-scenarios of their own, and so forth. As a matter of fact, most of the software test engineers will tell you that what makes their job so challenging is that it is very hard to cover all possible scenarios with tests. And because 100% test coverage is never possible, they need to cover what matters the most. But it often happens to be hard for a tester to narrow down the scope of their testing effort to "a subset of most critical scenarios", for a couple of reasons. First of all, due to often being disconnected from the rich customer context, it is really hard to say how does each scenario actually benefit the customer. (This can be a tough problem, as customer goals may represent a complex hierarchy of their own. The tester usually only has a very superficial knowledge of the real goals and it mainly comes from customer requirements and feedback, but not through thoroughly observing customer in their native environment.) Secondly, many scenarios are neither known nor easily discoverable in testing. It's not uncommon that new, unanticipated scenarios emerge from the execution environment that no one could have foreseen in development, even the customer themselves.

So, another category of assets to be cautious about is software systems with fractal value paths being user scenarios that they enable.

The last important category we will consider here is complex business workflows. Many business workflows consist of multiple different sub-workflows that are themselves made up of multiple workflows, and so on.

Certainly, more categories exist, but these three will give us an overall idea of how to answer the first question.

Now let's try to address the second question of how to determine the value of an asset that contains fractal value paths.

We have previously applied a pretty straightforward approach to assessing an asset value, consisting of the following conceptual steps:

1   Identify value paths

2   Score the value paths

3   Aggregate the scores

But we may end up with substantial inaccuracies using this method with assets having fractal value paths. Assigning a single numerical score to a composite value path may lead to a dramatic mismatch where the asset may rank high in capabilities that are irrelevant to the outcome (see Map 5-16). And this is hard to spot without exploring the subpaths of a path. One almost obvious solution is to "unpack" the paths: simply go a few levels down and score all the sub-sub-sub-...paths instead of just the high-level paths. Although this sounds very reasonable, the problem is that it would be a computational nightmare: if the asset had just four paths and each path had only four subpaths, and so on, then unpacking just two levels down would give us $4^3 = 64$ subpaths, and thus 64 scores to calculate.

But there's a better way that strikes a balance between the benefit of "unpacking" a composite path and avoiding an overwhelming number of calculations. We will call this approach *Pareto Unpacking*, as it selectively unpacks only the most impactful paths and subpaths. Let's see how it works in a very simple example.

Let's assume our asset has three value paths (P_1, P_2, P_3), and they are all fractal paths. First, we will score the importance of each path, but with percentages rather than unit-less integers. So, for example, the percentages for the three paths can be 15%, 75%, and 10% respectively. We will apply the Pareto principle and select the subpath, or subpaths, that produce about 80% of the value. In this case, it will be path P_2 that we unpack further while leaving the other two paths intact. If P_2 has three subpaths, P_α, P_β, and P_γ, we can now score these subpaths by importance, relative to one another, also in percentages. Let's say we get something like 25%, 60%, and 15%. At this point we will stop, assuming that going this far below the main paths will offer a decent level of improvement. To be able to perform the cross-level calculation, we will replace percentages everywhere with their decimal representations, meaning that instead of 15% we will use 0.15, and so on.

The most primitive expression for total value would be:

$0.15 \cdot C_1 + 0.75 \cdot C_2 + 0.1 \cdot C_3$ where C_1, C_2, and C_3 are capability scores for each of the three paths.

But we are going to substitute path P_2 with its subpaths and because of that capability score C_2 is substituted by:

$0.25 \cdot C_\alpha + 0.6 \cdot C_\beta + 0.15 \cdot C_\gamma$ where C_α, C_β, and C_γ are capability scores for corresponding subpaths of P_2.

After substituting this expression in place of C_2, we get:
$0.15 \cdot C_1 + 0.75 \cdot (0.25 \cdot C_\alpha + 0.6 \cdot C_\beta + 0.15 \cdot C_\gamma) + 0.1 \cdot C_3$

This is approximately equal to:
$0.15 \cdot C_1 + 0.19 \cdot C_\alpha + 0.45 \cdot C_\beta + 0.11 \cdot C_\gamma + 0.1 \cdot C_3$

So, we replaced our initial expression with one that better reflects the way our asset enables the outcome.

If we have multiple instances of the asset to choose from (perhaps different candidates for the same job, or different accounting software systems to replace a corporate legacy app), we would use a similar approach as before: score all asset instances in terms of their capability per each path and plug them into the expression we obtained. The only difference is that our calculations are now a lot more sensitive to the subpaths of the most impactful value paths, which will help protect us from making a wrong decision.

This unpacking process can continue down through the levels of subpaths when a more accurate analysis is needed, but it is important not to obsess with too much "accuracy", remembering that every path structure is just a model and every model has limits on how accurately it represents reality.

Assets with fractal value paths—or complex assets, as we called them earlier—are the exact opposite of commodities. A commodity is an asset that can be "plugged" into a system that utilizes it, but can actually be replaced by any other instance of that same commodity with no change to the outcome. Complex assets, on the other hand, cannot be easily replaced (or sometimes cannot be replaced at all). They strike their root deep into the system and in a sense, become an integral part of it. Commodity, on the other hand, could be described as a type of an asset with the same identical value path structure regardless of the origin or the producer of the asset.

Many organizations underestimate the complexity of an asset, making simplistic decisions that seem to assume one asset can be easily substituted for another. In other words, they tend to treat a complex asset as if it was a commodity. Some organizations treat people as completely fungible assets and fail to understand and leverage the real drivers of workforce productivity. Some treat software solutions as simple plug-and-play widgets which leads to uninformed buy vs. build decisions and is also the reason digital transformation efforts often fail.

A solid understanding of fractal value paths may help reveal performance bottlenecks in the organization. For example, an organization may be looking to hire more IT specialists with expertise in managing identity services, to address an apparent bottleneck for many software development tasks. But hiring another person, in addition to the four people already on staff, might not be helpful. Perhaps the real reason there is a bottleneck is that only one of four is actually able to help software development teams with their requests. While all four have good knowledge of identity services, only one had decent exposure and knowledge of the enterprise's IT ecosystem, and this is the only person developers can trust to make changes to the settings in identity services without breaking anything else in the vast enterprise application landscape. The value path of "knowing the ecosystem" and all of its numerous subpaths is the real culprit, rather than the "knowledge of identity services". This understanding might lead to a more productive strategy for dealing with the bottleneck, perhaps by helping the other three IT specialists acquire a better understanding of the ecosystem, maybe by pairing them with the knowledgeable team member on various tasks for a while, until they can operate on their own.

The value discovery process for complex assets (assets with fractal value paths) is:

1 *Identify value paths that connect the asset to its outcomes*

2 *Score the paths by importance*

3 *Identify subpaths of the most important paths (apply the Pareto 80/20 rule)*

4 *Unpack the most important paths in the formula for the total value*

Assets create value in complex ways involving many unknowns, which implies that:

The analysis must be coupled with probing (action aiming to reveal the unknowns). Any analysis or scoring of paths and subpaths remains hypothetical until empirical evidence can prove otherwise.

Versatile Assets

Questions about the value of assets like corporate culture, critical thinking, courage, psychological safety, motivation, and so on, are so complex that neither financial value nor relative value can be easily assessed. The *versatility of an asset* makes these questions so hard to answer. An asset is *versatile* if it enables multiple different outcomes at different levels on the outcome chain.

A versatile asset is usually not something material or tangible. In some sense, it's not a "thing" but rather a *manner* in which other assets produce value. And because of that, versatile assets serve as value moderators to other assets or value paths. Most of the time a versatile asset is fully intangible and adds value to the organization only through moderating the impact of more tangible assets. Versatile assets have tremendous influence over the outcome chain precisely because they are "plugged" into so many different points of impact:

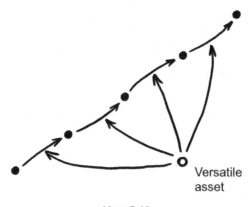

Map 5-18

We depict a versatile asset as a "transparent" node on the diagrams, emphasizing its intangible nature.

In Chapter 3 we used an example of an outcome chain for the complex task of establishing higher skill-set elasticity for software developers. An example of a high-impact versatile asset that moderates practically the entire chain is psychological safety:

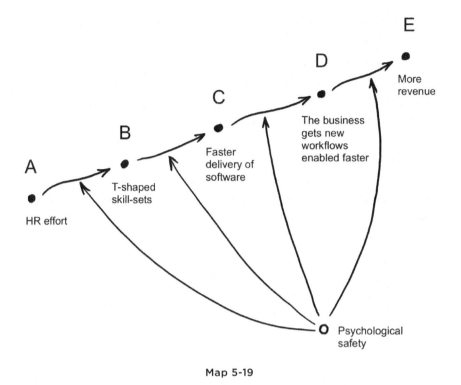

E

D

C

B

A

HR effort

T-shaped
skill-sets

Faster
delivery of
software

The business
gets new
workflows
enabled faster

More
revenue

O Psychological
safety

Map 5-19

The joint effort of the HR group and the management of the software development organization in fostering T-shaping among developers (the A-B link of the chain) is likely to result in no advancement whatsoever if there is no psychological safety for developers. The problem is that acquiring new skills (which is what T-shaping essentially is about) is hardly possible without trial and error but without psychological safety, the "error" part may be perceived as a source of future problems. (Even though errors are an inevitable part of any learning process, some environments give people reservations about revealing these errors, so the errors would not be brought up in the next performance review and held against them.) The B-C link is also contingent upon psychological safety. Even if new skills are acquired, it doesn't mean that people will be eager to use them if they feel their current role in the organization might be jeopardized. (Reassignment to a new area or role—even if positioned as temporary and for the purpose of T-shaping—will lead to anxiety as a person is less proficient in a newly acquired skill.) The C-D link needs psychological safety among the users of software being delivered. Adoption of a new release can be easily impeded by the danger of running into a problem with the management if using new software prevents users from fulfilling their routine responsibilities. And lastly, the D-E link is also moderated by psychological safety. The new workflows may open some opportunities to improve the ultimate business value for the organization but might be impeded by users' concerns that solving problems and handling operations in an unconventional manner might have repercussions.

We can use the following notation for simplicity or when multiple versatile assets are considered at the same time:

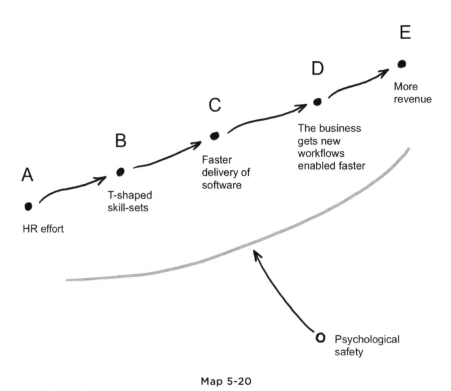

Map 5-20

It is virtually impossible to calculate the total value that a versatile asset creates across all levels of an outcome chain. In part, this is because comparing scores from different levels of a chain is a very difficult task. And that is why it is impossible to derive a single-number answer to a question of what's the value of culture, psychological safety, discipline or courage. It is much more feasible, however, to assess the impact of a versatile asset on a particular link in the outcome chain. Such an analysis is quite useful as it can easily translate into specific action.

Instead of asking a question we know we cannot answer, like "What's the value of psychological safety?" we will ask more specifically, "What's the value of psychological safety to T-shaping?" In other words, we are reducing the scope of the original question to just the A-B link of the chain:

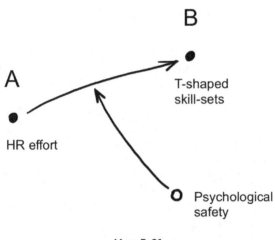

Map 5-21

To answer this question, let's "unpack" the A-B link into its high-level value paths and see how psychological safety "taps" into each of those paths for a particular enterprise context. Let's say the value paths and their relative importance scores are as follows:

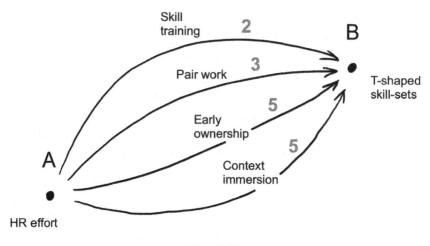

Map 5-22

Now let's score the relative impact our versatile asset produces on each of the value paths:

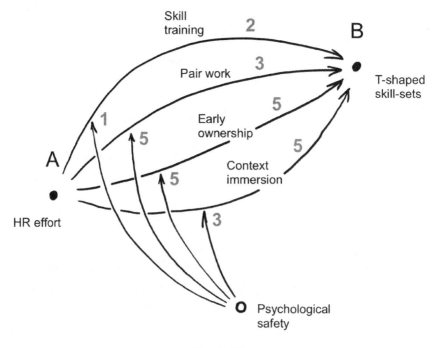

Map 5-23

Psychological safety has a low impact on skill training because it is usually easy to go to training, it doesn't require any subsequent action, and even people who feel psychologically unsafe in their environment would attend it and possibly learn something useful there. The impact on pair work is significantly higher. If Sunil wants to acquire a better practical understanding of a certain new skill and Josh is proficient in that skill, Josh might be an obvious candidate for Sunil to pair with on certain tasks. But if Josh has reasons to feel unsafe about his future (perhaps he suspects Sunil is being prepared to take over his role) or he has specific reasons to distrust management, he might be reluctant to engage in productive collaboration. Similarly, the influence of psychological safety on accepting early ownership over a task scores a 5 because if people feel they will be reprimanded for mistakes, they will avoid ownership of tasks involving the newly acquired skill-sets, and stick to tasks they know well which have a much smaller risk of mistakes or reprimands. Lastly, the impact on context immersion is 3 because if people feel judged for their lack of depth in the new skill, they will avoid exposing themselves to other teams and rely on their own efforts rather than learning through collaboration.

The product of the two scores for each value path reveals the total relative impact of psychological safety on the different value paths:

Versatile asset to paths	Skill training	Pair work	Early ownership	Context immersion
Psychological safety	2	15	25	15

"Fostering early ownership" is the aspect of psychological safety the organization's attention should be focussed on.

Similar "Pareto Unpacking" could be done here to explore the impact of psychological safety on early ownership by following the method like before.

The complexity of versatile assets is exacerbated by the fact that a lot of value paths transpire later in the process, either because they were not noticed from the very beginning or because they are emergent, and unfold only at a certain point in time. Analysis can only deal with known value paths, but the "known" portion of the impact of a versatile asset on the outcome can be too small to reliably represent the full landscape. Interaction with the environment is as important as the speculative analysis, if not more so.

The approach we have taken to explore the impact of versatile assets on a specific link in the outcome chain can be used in a very similar manner for assessing the impact of *any* value moderator.

The Dynamic Nature of Value Paths

Value paths of complex assets have another tricky property that must be taken into account: often they are dynamic in nature. It can be thought of as a complex web of Christmas lights where different segments light up at different times. Only unlike most of the Christmas lights that alternate on a certain preprogrammed pattern, fractal value paths may have no activation pattern at all, driven by a multitude of different interacting forces.

A software developer will have to use different facets of their skill depending on the nature of the work, perhaps their own creativity, programming style, implementation strategy, architecture, and so on. Their current task may heavily rely on creating new classes, utilizing inheritance to create a well-structured hierarchy of polymorphic system behavior, but the next task uses a completely different set of skills: building and debugging complicated data sorting and de-duping algorithms and persisting result-sets in the database.

There can be significant uncertainty in which value paths get activated, when, and for how long. Uncertainty has to be taken into account as a part of the value discovery process. To illustrate how inherent uncertainty influences value analysis, let's consider an extreme case based on the previously used example of hiring a marketing specialist. Only this time around we have learned that depending on which marketing campaign they are working on, any of the four skills can be critical or irrelevant and that "criticality" is equally distributed over their entire scope of anticipated campaigns in the upcoming quarter. In other words, instead of fixed importance factors for all campaign-related work (text copy: 8, graphics: 2, SEO: 2, and SMO: 5), we now get different numbers for different campaigns. For Campaign 1, text copy is almost irrelevant, but graphic design is everything, and this is also the reason for the big emphasis on SMO rather than SEO. In Campaign 2, the main emphasis is on SEO. The different campaigns have different importance scores that seem random:

Campaigns and importance factors	Text copy importance (Skill$_1$)	Graphics importance (Skill$_2$)	SEO importance (Skill$_3$)	SMO importance (Skill$_4$)
Campaign 1	2	7	1	5
Campaign 2	1	1	5	2
Campaign 3	5	2	1	3
...	...	...	...	...

If the scores are fully random, then over time all skills would contribute equally and no preference should be given to any one of the four skills. The most appropriate candidate scoring formula would simply be:

Candidate Score = Skill$_1$ + Skill$_2$ + Skill$_3$ + Skill$_4$.

Indeed, over the entire set of campaigns, each skill is crucial a roughly equal number of times and therefore all skills are equally needed. This is in contrast to our previous formula where we knew that different skills are contributing differently to the overall result.

In reality, however, some of the skills will have more stable demand (either high or low) and some will have variable demand, so some form of average must be taken over those value paths. Here's one way this can be incorporated in our calculations.

We need to find examples of campaigns with significantly different skill configurations required. Let's say it would be the following three:

Campaigns and importance factors	Text copy importance (Skill$_1$)	Graphics importance (Skill$_2$)	SEO importance (Skill$_3$)	SMO importance (Skill$_4$)
Campaign A	2	7	1	5
Campaign B	1	1	5	2
Campaign C	6	1	2	3

If this more or less covers the main possibilities, we will make a cosmetic, but important, change to the table, by replacing "Campaign A" with "Configuration A" and so on:

Campaigns and importance factors	Text copy importance (Skill$_1$)	Graphics importance (Skill$_2$)	SEO importance (Skill$_3$)	SMO importance (Skill$_4$)
Configuration A	2	7	1	5
Configuration B	1	1	5	2
Configuration C	6	1	2	3

This emphasizes the fact that all our campaigns, to our knowledge, roughly split into three classes of campaigns, each represented by one skill *configuration*. We will call these rows a *complete set* of asset configurations.

We need to know how likely it is that a campaign will have a configuration similar to A, B or C. Expressed as simple percentages, let's assume:

Campaigns and importance factors	Likelihood	Text copy importance (Skill$_1$)	Graphics importance (Skill$_2$)	SEO importance (Skill$_3$)	SMO importance (Skill$_4$)
Configuration A	60%	2	7	1	5
Configuration B	15%	1	1	5	2
Configuration C	25%	6	1	2	3

In other words, around 60% of campaigns require skill configurations similar to A, 15% similar to B, and 25% similar to C.

This information allows us to calculate an "average score" for each skill according to their corresponding likelihood. The average for Skill$_1$ would be:

Skill$_1$ = 0.6·2 + 0.15·1 + 0.25·6 = 2.85.

After performing calculations for every skill, we get:

Campaigns and importance factors	Likelihood	Text copy importance (Skill$_1$)	Graphics importance (Skill$_2$)	SEO importance (Skill$_3$)	SMO importance (Skill$_4$)
Configuration A	60%	2	7	1	5
Configuration B	15%	1	1	5	2
Configuration C	25%	6	1	2	3
Average:	-	2.85	4.6	1.85	4.05

When assessing a new candidate for the marketing specialist job, it would make sense to use the total score formula, reflecting the dynamic nature of workload that the candidate would have to deal with:

Candidate Score = 2.85·Skill$_1$ + 4.6·Skill$_2$ + 1.85·Skill$_3$ + 4.05·Skill$_4$.

So, tho summarize this approach in a more general case...

In the case of dynamic value path behavior, the value discovery process is as follows:

1   *Identify the value paths connecting the asset to the outcome*

2   *Find a complete set of asset configurations*

3   *Determine the approximate likelihood of each configuration*

4   *Find the average importance scores of each value path using configurations and their percentage likelihood*

5   *Calculate the scores across all paths to find the overall asset value*

Caution must be taken here. Often times path variability may not be seen at the highest-level paths but is rather hidden within them. A software developer may need to do about 50% business logic programming and 50% database work, but underneath these high-level paths might be a completely random activation of various subpaths. The seemingly stable 50% database work may involve creating indices for one task but then tweaking field validation rules and triggers for the other. Another task might all be performance-tuning of the SQL queries. These are very different types of activities, which means that the analysis in such cases may require some high-impact value paths to be "unpacked".

The complex behavior of fractal value paths in a complex asset might activate over time like this:

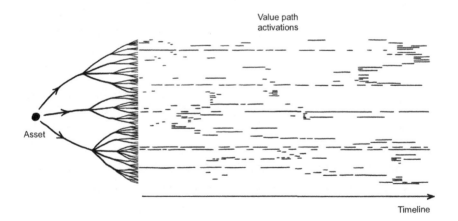

Map 5-24

It looks like Guitar Hero on steroids. Different subpaths activate at different times, new paths and subpaths emerge, and the old ones expire. The complex behavior of such assets demonstrates that it is so dangerous to think of complex assets the same way as commodities.

Nonlinear Value

In less complex examples of value paths, the "yield" of value might be close to linear. For example, the more product distribution channels you get, the more revenue you would receive, so twice as many channels might give you roughly twice the amount of revenue.

This is not true in more complex situations. Many value paths are *nonlinear* in nature, which means that the change in input of a value path does not produce a proportional change in yield. While there is a countless number of various nonlinear behaviors, we will primarily be looking at two common types of nonlinear value yield:

1 Progressive yield
2 Regressive yield

Progressive yield is the case when the increase in value grows faster than the increase in inputs:

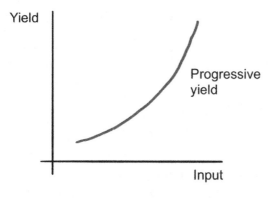

Map 5-25

Regressive yield is when the increase in value grows more slowly than the increase in inputs.

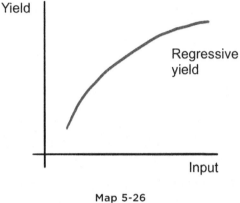

Map 5-26

For progressive yield, it is easy to see that the same increment in input produces a smaller increment of yield early on, but a greater increment later:

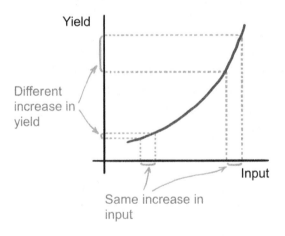

Map 5-27

For a regressive yield, the same increment of input produces a greater increment in yield at the beginning but a smaller yield further on:

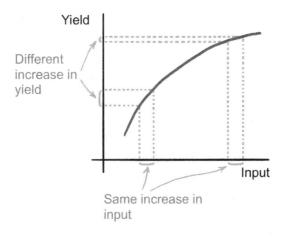

Map 5-28

Exponential growth is one example of a progressive yield, but of course, there are others. As for regressive yield, you may have heard the expression: "diminishing returns". That's exactly what regressive yield is about.

One example of progressive yield would be social reviews of products. The asset in this case is the social network of customers who actively participate in reviewing products: writing reviews, rating a product, or rating other customers' comments. When this active subset of customers is small, very few products have reviews and the effect on sales revenue is minimal. But as the network grows, more and more products receive multiple reviews, ratings, and ratings of reviews, creating an increasing confidence in buyers that they are making an informed decision, and so sales improve more and more significantly.

An example of a regressive yield would be optimizing the performance of a software system to improve user experience. At first, when the application is fairly slow, making the application work faster leads to a significant increase in user satisfaction. But as the application gets faster and faster, the user cares less and less.

One of the reasons we have used a linear scale in our examples so far is that modeling nonlinear behavior is not easy. Also, empirical evidence is needed to reveal whether a value path shows regressive or progressive behavior, and this needs to be probed for. With all that in mind, the nonlinear behavior of value yield is sometimes too impactful to be ignored and requires a more sophisticated approach. Assume we have a value path with an importance score of 5, relative to other value paths, and we assess the asset capability down this path as 3. But instead of just multiplying 5 by 3, we are going to make some additional operations. If this path has a progressive yield, then the asset capability of 3 needs to be amplified, and if the path has a regressive yield, it must be attenuated. A relatively simple way to do this is to apply a power function to 3, using a power greater than 1 for a progressive yield, and a power between 0 and 1 for a regressive yield.

Here's an example of calculations for a nonlinear yield, regressive in this case. An organization wants to purchase a well-rounded database management system to replace an old one. "Well-rounded" means that preference will be given to products having *all* the desired features at a decent level while avoiding solutions focussed more on one type of task and not supporting others. The company might be using these parameters as criteria:

1   Effective support for debase clusters
2   Easy backups
3   Flexible indexing model
4   Effective encryption/decryption of data
5   Advanced transaction support

We will use the following formula for the product's total score:
Product Score = $(\text{Cluster})^{0.01}$ + $(\text{Backup})^{0.01}$ + $(\text{Indexing})^{0.01}$ + $(\text{Encryption})^{0.01}$ + $(\text{Transactions})^{0.01}$.

This uses a function with a quickly regressing yield by raising the number to power 0.01, which can be calculated easily in any spreadsheet software, for example. Now, let's assume the organization considered two solutions, Database X and Database Y, with the following scores:

Candidate	Cluster	Backup	Indexing	Encryption	Transactions
Database X	2	2	2	2	2
Database Y	1	10	1	1	1

Using the data from these two rows in the formula will provide these results:

Candidate	Cluster	Backup	Indexing	Encryption	Transactions	Total
Database X	2	2	2	2	2	5.035
Database Y	1	10	1	1	1	5.023

This means that Database X is the preferred choice.

(Note that when using formulas approximating a regressive yield—diminishing returns—even a small difference signifies a *substantial* distinction between the solution options.)

If we had used a simple linear expression instead of the regressive formula, the preference would have to be given to Database Y with a score of 14 points, instead of Database X with only 10 points. And that would certainly be a poor choice.

Systematic Probing for Value

Any aspect of value is just a hypothesis unless proven differently. Besides, complex assets, as we've already witnessed, may contain a significant amount of unknown unknowns. A good probing methodology is needed to effectively deal with the missing pieces. Otherwise, the organization ends up navigating in the wrong direction at a great expense, trusting that something is value when in fact it isn't.

Assume we have an asset that we believe enables a certain outcome through value paths with some scores of importance and capability, respectively. We want to uncover the answers to these two main questions:

Question 1: Do those outcomes, value paths, and scores correspond to reality?

Question 2: Are there any missing outcomes or value paths?

Both direct and indirect probing methods discussed in the previous chapter apply here. An approximation of the asset might activate some value paths and demonstrate whether the assumptions about their corresponding scores were correct. It may also reveal previously unknown value paths or help discover new outcomes that weren't obvious before. Value moderators quite often can only be discovered by probing, and direct probing is good for that purpose, as a good approximation of the future state of the system may also point to key parameters governing the achievement of the outcome. Similarly, the substitution method can reveal new aspects of value as a part of indirect discovery.

True vs. False Economic Choices

We've been talking about value as a means of finding a better economic choice, but it's important to be able to tell a true economic choice from an apparent one. We can use this knowledge to leverage better economic options where they are readily available, but also to try to make the best choice possible even when it's not obvious at first glance.

Our main examples here will relate to an enterprise e-commerce system. We want to know where we should invest:

1   In creating the system's user interface, or the system's database?

2   In integration with a third party loyalty program, or in electronic gift cards?

The first question represents a *false* economic choice, for quite an obvious reason: a user interface is pointless without a database, and vice versa. So, regardless of which option has been selected, no economic value is achieved. The second choice is a meaningful one, as either option has the potential of generating value.

It is important to keep in mind that enterprise tasks are not always economically comparable, even if they are supposed to be performed by the same unit or team.

But what is even more interesting is that sometimes a question can be restated to represent a meaningful economic choice, but that new choice must be made in a different dimension than originally selected. In Question 1, instead of selecting which *layer* of the system to implement, we go in an orthogonal direction and compare *meaningful features* to one another. Most of the features will require work on both UI and Database and that's the reason why we call them "orthogonal". And deciding between two properly defined features may actually be a legitimate economic choice.

So, what was the root of the error in Question 1?

Here it is. Just because something incurs cost, doesn't imply it generates meaningful value. To make an economic choice between two options, both options have to represent meaningful value.

Sometimes an organization has to fundamentally alter the way it thinks of assets or redefine what it considers as assets. If both a user interface and a database are considered assets then any meaningful value analysis will be very hard to convey because neither represents standalone value. If the organization looks at application *features* as assets instead, then it can have a meaningful conversation about value and economic choices.

This generally applies to all kinds of assets, not only to software: in order to be able to make meaningful and sufficiently granular economic decisions, assets need to be thought of as something that can produce a meaningful outcome. Otherwise, it is very difficult to reason about the value.

Organizational fragmentation negatively influences a company's ability to achieve outcomes, getting stuck in numerous disconnects instead. As it has been noted in previous chapters, fragmentation negatively influences both outcome focus and the ability to uncover unknowns.

Outcome Ownership and Value Discovery

We can expand the list of responsibilities for the outcome owner with respect to value:

Outcome Owner
Responsibilities related to managing value
Facilitate the value discovery process. This often requires to: • Identify critical assets that contribute to your outcomes • For an asset, determine value paths, subpaths, and their respective scores • Identify value moderators and their influence on assets and value paths • Ensure proper treatment of complex assets and their fractal value paths • Aggregate the pieces into a consistent, integrated understanding of value for a given asset. Understand how options influence value, and where there are opportunities to increase value.
Communicate asset value, and the way the value is achieved, to other participants of the process
Establish the means for empirical evidence to support or disprove the anticipated value
Interact with other outcome owners on the outcome chain to assist them (and to get assistance) with managing value

The mechanics of achieving most of these functions involves other people and puts the outcome owner, to a significant extent, in the role of the facilitator, communicator, and integrator of knowledge about the value.

The Way You Define Value Influences Value

The question of value can be politically loaded in some organizations. This is understandable as a higher perceived value provided by a unit often grants a wide range of positional advantages. It may become a lot easier to negotiate budgets or other resources when your unit delivers higher value, and it may serve as a stepping stone to a higher rank.

So, value, as perceived by the organization, impacts incentives, personal aspirations, and politics. It works the other way around, too, that incentives, personal aspirations, and politics all shape the understanding of value in the organization.

Leaders at different levels are often keen to know what business value they deliver precisely for this reason. And to some extent this coupling is very natural and, despite its negative side-effects, can never be entirely eliminated. It's important for an enterprise to avoid extremes and not allow business value to become a hostage of organizational politics, where value is defined to best suit career aspirations at the cost of actual benefit to the business.

The first sign of a problem is when an organization doesn't have a reliable mechanism for acquiring empirical evidence that could prove or disprove the realization of value as a result of a complex task. Some deeply pathological organizational learning dysfunctions have already been considered in Chapters 3 and 4.

Expressing value in financial terms also has a significant side-effect. It might be easier to reason about the value of an asset in financial terms, but this also comes with significant danger. Some assets may be so far removed from the ultimate organizational outcomes that it is virtually impossible to derive credible monetary values for them. This does not mean the assets are not valuable, only that their value is hard to express clearly in terms of revenue. But the difficulty in corresponding an asset with such a measure may play a nasty trick: it may simply devalue the asset in the eyes of the organization. The "rationale" is quite straightforward. Imagine that you have two assets: A and B. Asset A has a business value

PURSUING ENTERPRISE OUTCOMES

of $5 million. The value of Asset B is hard to say. We'll invest in Asset A, for obvious reasons. The interesting part is that Asset B may end up being a lot more valuable. That, however, doesn't matter because not only its value cannot be compared to $5, 000, 000 at the moment of making the investment decision, but sometimes even post facto. And if you don't see the value of Asset B proactively, you probably won't see it retroactively either: your organization is simply unable to comprehend a different dimension of value.

That being said, however, extreme focus on the monetary expression of value may be dictated not as much by myopia, as by the need for strict fiscal discipline. When the value of an asset is hard to express in money, it may inspire creative justifications for completely useless things, which can drain a significant amount of an organization's resources. Some organizations will have learned the hard way that it's better for them to stick to monetary values only. Even though this argument is understandable, it is not a good way to go about value. First of all, there's plenty of abuse of financial measures, too. Benefits that are promised in hard financial terms may easily fail to be delivered. Additionally, organizations often have an established mechanism in place to retroactively "dampen the expectations" when idyllic business plans hit a harsh reality. Secondly, it is hugely irresponsible to overlook the value only because it is not conveniently representable in financial terms. As we've seen throughout the chapter, the value of some assets is very hard to express in terms of money and yet it may be a highly impactful asset, as in case of versatile assets, for example. Effective probing is needed as a core organizational discipline to ensure that lower-level outcomes are being achieved and value is being created in appropriate forms and shapes.

What Constitutes Ultimate Value?

We've talked a lot about intermittent outcomes because they were a handy tool for assessing the value of an asset. In fact, we mostly dealt with immediate outcomes on the outcome chain, going further up the outcome chain only when we had to compare assets that bear significantly distinct functions that make them incomparable directly (the "apples to oranges" case). In that case, we were trying to find the closest common outcome, and assess value against that. We also learned that there can be multiple different outcomes at a certain level, not just one. Oftentimes, the value discovery process can reveal previously unknown outcomes.

And only in a few instances—like in Doug's example—have we looked at the ultimate value the organization is creating, which was revenue in that case. It was a rare case because usually assets are situated far away from the ultimate outcome on the outcome chain, having multiple degrees of separation from it.

But the question of ultimate organizational value still matters because it is the ultimate criterion for the utility of everything else in the enterprise. Although most of the assets cannot be assessed directly against ultimate outcomes, the nature of those outcomes still influences the process of value discovery and delivery. One such crucial aspect is the multiplicity of ultimate outcomes. We've so far adopted a simple stance with regard to ultimate outcomes, focusing on revenue, but this simplification can be too far from the truth to be useful, so we need to expand on this a little.

Here's a simple example of an outcome that transcends revenue in its most simplistic form. Doug, the CEO from our earlier example, is considering a new partnership deal. He has two options:

1   Company X, another good distributor that could add more market reach for Doug's product

2   Company Y, specializing in product development. Company Y would not help sell any products but it could help Doug's organization build a whole new value proposition.

Should Doug invest his company's effort and money with Company X or Company Y?

Clearly, "current revenue" is insufficient criteria to make such a decision. In this case, we need to decide between two ultimate outcomes: Current Revenue and Future Revenue. This is a particularly interesting assessment process because:

- Company X can only contribute to Current Revenue while Company Y can only contribute to Future Revenue. Some way is needed to compare across the two outcomes.

- While it is clear what revenue can be expected from the partnership with Company X, it is uncertain what revenue could be generated in partnership with Company Y.

How can current and future revenues be compared to each other? There is a standard answer to that in net present value (or NPV). The idea is simply that a dollar available today is more valuable than a dollar that will be available only in the future because the dollar available today could be reliably invested (using some universally available investment mechanisms with predictable interest rate) by the time the other dollar becomes available. This approach of comparison of current and future cash flows—however tempting—is misleading when considered in the enterprise context, because it's not only the money that matters but also *what* generates it.

Imagine two corporations: Corporation L and Corporation M. Corporation L has a very strong current cash flow but behind the gloss of high revenue and margin lies a dark secret: the company has no real plans for the future. The product that it sells today is a big cash cow but it will expire in time and stagnation will follow. Corporation M is starving in terms of revenue today but has plenty of ideas and even early implementations of some future products. For Corporation L, every dollar that could be made in the future is actually of *higher* (not lower!) value than the current cash flow. For Corporation M, money today is of a much higher value than future cash flow. The two companies have very different takes on current vs. future revenue. Ultimate enterprise outcomes have to be carefully analyzed with respect to how they correlate with one another. Corporation L would conclude that working towards future growth is of higher importance to them than working towards revenue today, which they have an abundance of anyways. Corporation L would place relative scores as:

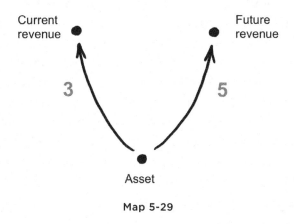

Map 5-29

Assets that can contribute to future revenues will be automatically valued higher than those which generate cash flow today.

The second complication comes from a much higher level of uncertainty of future cash flow compared to today, so experimentation and research are needed to uncover unknowns and work towards a better understanding of value.

Gluing It All Together

We have seen numerous examples and tools for value discovery. It's time to consolidate what we've learned in the form of key recommendations which could be used as "filters" to go through to determine what tool to use and how to use it in your context.

1   Before performing any value discovery, answer the question, "What is it for?" You need to be clear about the value of the

assets in question and *how the value will be used* once it has been figured out. What type of decisions will it support? It is highly recommended to imagine that you have the answer, any answer, even a fake answer, and then figure out what you would do with it. Is it going to be used to compare one asset to another and thus help decide which one to purchase/support/develop? Or will it be used to understand how actual value differs from potential higher values and thus whether an improvement action should be taken? Or is the idea to seek alternative solutions or even strategies? Whatever the case, would that "mock" answer be enough? Would it support the intended decision-making? If so, proceed to the actual value discovery. If not, further refine what you want to achieve with the knowledge of the asset's value once it is figured out, or change the way in which you seek to express value so that it would inform your decisions better.

2   At this point, you know what assets you are seeking to assess the business value of, and what you are going to do with that business value once it has been figured out. Now you must understand the outcome chain where the value occurs. It may be difficult to model out the entire outcome chain, from the assets in question all the way to ultimate organizational outcomes, but you need to have a chain that shows at least a few levels of outcomes beyond your immediate outcomes. Without that extra depth, you are in danger of over-optimizing for immediate outcomes at the cost of higher-order ones.

3   Next, you need to understand where the main bulk of the discovery process will be – at what level of the outcome chain. You might need to focus on the immediate outcome or the closest common one, depending on whether the assets being compared perform the same, similar or different functions. It would also be helpful to clarify whether you are dealing with a single specific outcome or a number of outcomes at that level. Either way, these will be the criteria for assessing value.

4   Next comes the process of identifying the value paths – the links connecting the assets in question to the selected outcomes. The discovery of value paths might not be a trivial matter and is most effectively done by combining speculative analysis with probing and empirical evidence. The process of value path discovery often reveals new paths connecting the assets to new outcomes.

5   Next, you need to determine whether the most feasible way to score value paths is in absolute measure of some kind, or in relative terms. It might make sense to score in absolute units of measure like money, customer conversions, or leads generated if each value path can independently produce some quantity of the unit and if the outcomes allow for a numerical measure. When the outcomes are not easily supported by a numerical value of some sort or when value paths do not produce meaningful quantities independently of each other, relative, unit-less scoring should be used.

6   Scoring requires careful treatment, whether in absolute or relative terms and often probing will also be required.

7   To understand the overall value of the asset, value for each of the paths has to be aggregated. For absolute measures, simply add up each path's value score. For relative value, two scores need to be defined for each path: an importance score showing how important the path is to the outcome and a capability score showing how good the asset is in generating impact down this particular value path.

8   If it appears that some (or all) value paths are fractal, a more refined aggregation approach may need to be taken based on Pareto Unpacking.

9   If some value paths show (or are expected to show) volatile behavior, average values should be calculated based on key path configurations and their relative likelihood.

10   If some paths are expected to manifest nonlinear behavior, the path value for these paths should be calculated using some nonlinear functions; a power function, for example.

11 Moderators should be carefully analyzed for value paths. It is important to keep in mind that some moderators (or their actual effect on value) may not objectively reveal themselves other than through a fair amount of probing and experimentation.

12 Value discovery does not end here. The actual delivery of value and empirical evidence of its realization is what will continually refine the understanding of value, and support better decisions.

The cornerstone of our analysis was the concept of *value paths*. They are the key mechanism for acquiring the "next level of detail" regarding the business value of an asset. It is absolutely natural that most of the conversations pertaining to value discovery, revolve around the notion of value paths.

🫂 Taking Action

1   Take inventory of the complex assets you want to determine the business value of. (Select 2-3 of those where the need to determine value feels most pressing.)

2   Determine the *purpose* you are pursuing by exploring value for these assets. (Identify the reason you need to know the value, using the bullets: Effective funding, Opportunity to add more value, Finding alternative solutions. The motivation for value discovery can be different from the three areas described above. Either way, it has to be specified.)

3   For a given asset, build the outcome chain to which it contributes value. (Determine the immediate outcomes and higher-order outcomes as far as you know.)

4   Determine value paths and use them to calculate the value score. (To achieve this, break down the link between the asset and its immediate outcome into value paths. Try scoring asset capabilities and importance for each value path. Aggregate the results as described in the chapter, for the total value score. Use this score for value discovery, defined above. All of the scenarios involve comparing some alternatives and choosing the best one. Make sure you know what is being compared to what. If there's no comparison involved, then there's no reason for calculating any score.)

5   Refine your analysis using advanced tools. (For that, consider using other tools described in the chapter, such as identifying value moderators, applying Pareto Unpacking, utilizing non-linear value expression, assessing dynamic value using path configurations, and so on.)

6   Validate assumptions. (Plan the first step that would help you probe for value or empirically validate your assumptions about value. Without empirical input, it is only a hypothesis.)

CHAPTER 6

Complex Bottlenecks and Emergent Solutions

Simple vs. Complex Bottlenecks

Imagine you are the logistics manager of an online retail company, doing your best to maintain reliable operations. One day, demand for some of your products spikes significantly and grows from day to day. Your supply quickly vanishes. Your warehouse space was appropriate for the previous demand profile but wasn't able to cope with a sudden change in demand.

We can refer to warehouse space as a "bottleneck" for your company that has "blocked" the desired outcome of serving all customer requests. More warehouse space must be provided to "unblock" operations and enable the outcome.

The concept of a bottleneck is very useful when dealing with simple tasks. Bottlenecks can be identified, and either eliminated or mitigated leading to improved outcomes. Once a bottleneck is removed, something else becomes the bottleneck holding the company's performance back.

Things change, however, once we move away from simple tasks. Let's look at the marketing department of an insurance company. The organization wants to foster a more innovative approach to marketing in order to achieve a broader market share. But inspirational memos from management have not made any difference, and neither has training on "how to be more innovative in your workplace". When the leadership finally decided to conduct an anonymous survey, it revealed that employees lacked basic psychological safety around innovation. Innovation always contains a degree of risk, but in the past, the organization had reprimanded a couple of creative employees for deviating from a plan. Everyone had quickly learned that following the plan was always a safer option, even when it was known to be wrong. As a result, mediocre plans were followed unquestioned. No risky ideas were ever entertained. Esoteric reasons could always be found to explain subpar performance of marketing campaigns; all to the detriment of innovation.

Although it is not a bottleneck in a conventional sense, we can say that psychological safety acts as a bottleneck in achieving the organization's desired outcome of innovative marketing. For the retailer, warehouse space was a commodity that simply had to be supplied in sufficient quantity to create the desired operational capacity. The marketing department of the insurance company is dealing with a *complex bottleneck* representing a complex, intangible asset that enables a favorable outcome through a variety of sophisticated scenarios.

Some examples of complex bottlenecks are:

1   Poor discipline in business processes.

2   Distrust of management limiting employee productivity.

3   Lack of customer awareness hindering product sales.

4   Lack of test automation blocking a software development process.

5   Poor user experience with IT systems impacting business processes.

6 Sustained conflict limiting executive team productivity.

7 High attrition preventing expertise development.

8 Lack of skills limiting team performance.

A complex bottleneck always influences the outcome in multiple ways, unlike simple bottlenecks. For example, chronic conflict on the executive team can manifest as:

- Important initiatives remaining unapproved
- Critical assessment of capital initiatives being held in an unfair and unconstructive way
- Different branches of the organization being unable to cooperate productively toward a higher-level objective
- Difficulties in effectively allocating people and material resources

Each of these aspects splits into a number of sub-areas. The problem with critical assessments of large-scale initiatives manifests as:

- Hard to question anything, as it is immediately perceived as a personal threat
- No indicator is trusted by the team, even if the measurement has reasonable validity
- No substantial corrective action can be agreed upon, as it often goes against someone's expectations
- Team members can't think productively during meetings because of constant, grueling stress.

These bullets, in turn, split into sub-bullets and so on ad infinitum, as the figure shows:

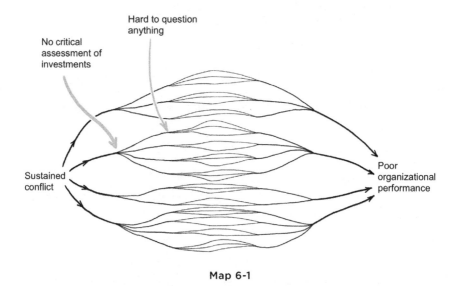

Map 6-1

A complex bottleneck has fractal paths and requires a complex asset to solve the problem.

Solutions to Complex Bottlenecks

Addressing a simple bottleneck is straightforward: supply the required quantity of a certain commodity resource and the bottleneck is addressed, allowing something else to become the system's next bottleneck. The system is now performing at a higher level because the previous bottleneck has been addressed.

Addressing a complex bottleneck requires a *complex solution*. Paradoxically, a complex solution can often be described in just a few words. The solutions to the complex bottlenecks above are:

1   Good work disciplinwe
2   Trust established with management
3   Strong customer awareness
4   Good test automation
5   User familiarity with the system

6 Productive collaboration

7 High employee retention

8 Advanced skill-sets.

Each solution sounds simple but is a complex mechanism dependent on very sophisticated behaviors.

The centerpiece of a complex solution is *human behavior* and "developing" a solution means developing that behavior. "Good work discipline" is a behavioral trait. Similarly, "trusting leadership" requires and implies a certain type of behavior. Despite the fact that "good test automation" seems to be a matter of technology, the key is really the team's ability to use and maintain the automated tests, and to be able to catch defects in their code. All eight of our examples above require a complex solution, with human behavior at the core. That also makes every such solution largely intangible. No wonder complex solutions are hard to deal with.

Of course, besides the solution core, there also are things that enable the solution. Certain corporate policies may serve as enablers to employee retention. A marketing campaign is an enabler to customer awareness, and so on. But it is important to not confuse what's primary and what's secondary in a solution. A corporate policy *isn't* a solution to high attrition. The solution is the behavior and the mindset of employees who prefer to stay and build their careers with the company rather than seek better opportunities elsewhere. The policy—no matter how appealing it may sound on paper—might not improve retention at all, or might backfire, causing higher attrition than before. Similarly, a marketing campaign is not the solution but just an enabler for the solution. The solution is the customer's strong conviction that this branded product is a good choice, resulting in customer action to purchase the product.

A complex solution is, first and foremost, human behavior. Enablers of a complex solution (such as software and hardware systems, policies, rules, etc.) are just factors that may support the solution but are not the solution itself.

Complex solution

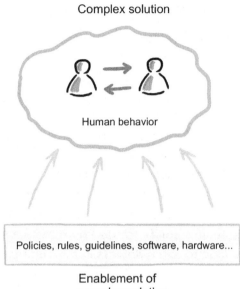

Human behavior

Policies, rules, guidelines, software, hardware...

Enablement of
complex solution

Map 6-2

The distinction is so important because it is so easy to believe that a software application or career guidance or a marketing campaign will make problems drop away and everything will just fall into place. The stark distinction between output and outcome examined in Chapter 3 amply demonstrates and explains why this is not the case.

How can a complex solution come into existence?

It seems obvious that we can just design the solution so that it addresses the bottleneck. But the main problem is that human behavior cannot be "designed to a specification". Let's consider an example to illustrate this.

The management of a company facing "poor discipline in business processes" is quite eager to "create" the right amount of discipline by any possible means. They follow the most obvious path and simply mandate in a politely worded memo that discipline violations will be punished. If your tasks aren't completed on time, or you don't produce work of a certain quality, there will be negative career consequences. On the other hand, anyone with a great work discipline will be rewarded with more successful careers.

For some time, with fewer issues around work discipline, the management is happy, but then projects begin to run hopelessly behind schedule, and items are shipped to the customer in a horrible condition. The management pushes harder, giving a clear directive to local team leaders to police any violation of delivery discipline, but the situation doesn't improve. Nothing appears to threaten the project outcome until it suddenly becomes clear the outcome is not going to be achieved. Most importantly, the complex bottleneck of poor work discipline remains unresolved because punitive measures were an attempt to "design" the solution and led to adverse effects. People started gaming the rules reporting overly optimistic status, and because of the complex nature of projects, this created an impression of temporary relief, when it was just the "calm before the storm".

Similarly, the other complex bottlenecks in our list would not be addressed by demanding certain behavior or supplying a "sufficient amount" of constrained matter. The solution to the bottleneck is too complex to be *designed*, but it can *emerge* if the right supporting mechanisms are brought into action.

How Solutions Emerge

The only way by which new behaviors appear in a complex environment is through the process of emergence. Behaviors cannot be simply changed to match a specific expectation. The previous example demonstrated quite well what happens when we try to "override" natural forces of the environment instead of leveraging them. A whole different, unexpected, and, most importantly, unfavorable scenarios had emerged.

Behaviors in a complex system can only emerge. Any attempt to "design" behavior to match a specific expectation will only result in waste.

185

What would a *favorable* emergence path look like?

Let's consider three emergent solutions that evolve toward successful outcomes.

Example 1. *Trust in leadership*

A department struggles to innovate their systems and the services they deliver. The reason behind this struggle is that employees have no faith in their management. Over several years, if anything ever went wrong with any piece of innovation, the employees originating the innovation would be thrown under the bus by their own management. As a result, a defensive behavior has emerged: keep your head down and don't draw attention to yourself by taking risks.

Peter, a manager from another department, is moved over to lead one of the groups in this problem unit. People trust each other in Peter's former department, so when he sees the situation with his new teams he decides to act on it. His first step is an open and honest conversation with the teams, but the teams seem disinterested in repairing trust, and no one opens up about their problems. Disappointed but not discouraged, Peter tries one-on-one sessions with his new team members. Most of these are unhelpful, as team members remain reluctant to disclose any of their problems or actual feelings, but a few do share how they feel about taking on any improvement or innovation activities and why. This is enough for Peter to get a rough idea of the situation.

Two days later, he gathers everyone and apologizes for the way they have been treated in the past by his predecessors. No promises are made, no blame is laid, but he articulates his understanding of how they must have felt being put in such a position. And just before closing the meeting, he throws in an incidental request:

"Guys, I'd like you to think of what improvement opportunities you've had in mind but have held off. Pick one or two, add them to your backlog, and assign yourself and me as owners."

For days after the meeting, there are quiet conversations among team members about how much they can trust this new boss, and what his previous teams were like.

Ultimately, some team members decide they will give it a shot. Over the next couple of weeks, two items are identified, and Peter asks to meet with each of the item owners to determine impediments and risks. The team members flesh out what they anticipate as potential hurdles, and Peter takes note of some action items to help resolve those impediments. Peter notices that the way the two improvement items were formulated was overly focused on what needs to be done rather than what the result of that effort will be. He decides to take this up with them and allocate some time to collaboratively determine what those tasks actually aim to improve. But both task owners feel like they are being doubted, so their enthusiasm begins to falter. Peter takes care not to cross the line but wants to achieve some clarity on the anticipated results of the tasks. He ultimately runs a little simulation with the two of them to alleviate the tension:

Peter: "Guys, I'm going to ask you to participate in a little thought experiment with me. Each of you, imagine that you are the head of a large unit."

Guys (Natalie and Chris), intrigued by their imaginary roles, decide to play along.

Peter: "What are your primary objectives?"

Natalie: "To make sure that the department is productive ... that it delivers value ..."

Peter: "Okay, good goal. It's a little vague, but it will do for now. And what constraints are you operating under?"

Chris: "Money!"

Natalie: "Not just money though. Budgets are one thing. There's also time ..."

Peter: "Okay, money, time. Anything else?"

Natalie shrugs her shoulders and Chris seems to be thinking deeply.

Peter: "Alright, money and time it is. So, what does it mean for you to be a good unit leader? What do you actually have to do, given the goal and the constraint."

Natalie: "I need to make sure that the budget and time are used to deliver things that represent maximum value, I guess ..."

Peter: "Chris?"

Chris: "Well, besides the fact that the problem is always in the details of how to actually do it, conceptually I agree with what Natalie said."

Peter: "Perfect. So, Chris, following on from your point of how to actually use money and time effectively to drive value, what do you think would help?"

Chris: "It would help to explore my unit's scope of work a bit deeper in terms of whether—"

Natalie: "Oh! That's such a setup!" She smiles and continues: "Chris, don't you see where he's going with this?"

Chris: "Ha! But it actually makes sense. You do need to know what exactly an improvement action aims at. Otherwise, you may be wasting your money."

Natalie: "... and time. We got it, boss. We got it." They go over the details of the outcomes their improvement activities are aiming at, which helps shed some light on their plan with each item. And at the next team planning session, the two items are taken by the team. Natalie and Chris have more confidence now and can work more productively with Peter. They even feel a touch of guilt about doubting his intentions when he asked them to clarify the goals of each task, and are now more eager to seek ways to collaborate productively.

As the work progresses over the course of the month, Peter successfully removes some of the impediments he promised to address, which he reports to Natalie and Chris. He is only stuck with one item on his list, but he reports the actual status to the team in just the same way. This creates a good impression of honesty and transparency on most of the team members, except for Chris. It was Chris' task, and although he is not happy, he is comfortable enough to challenge whether Peter had been pushing hard enough to resolve the impediment that is blocking his task. This immediately catches everyone's attention, as challenging a group leader had been unthinkable. Peter is slightly annoyed by so much radical candor, but he instantly recognizes an opportunity. Peter quickly facilitates a new plan, devised by the whole team, to mitigate the impact of the remaining impediment based on the team's new idea.

By the end of the month, Natalie's item gets completed and Chris' item is still in progress but looks promising. But then, even though Natalie's task seemed to be successfully completed, it caused some headaches for teams on the user support side in another department. The group that discovers the problem complains about Peter's unit. Peter immediately puts his team to work solving the issue, making sure to not make a bigger deal out of the complaint than it already is. Within two days the problem is identified and fixed. It turns out a wrong connection type was preventing the support group from performing bulk data operations. When the solution is verified, Peter finally has a detailed conversation with his management. They are ready to crucify him, as their bosses have heard about the problem and are expecting some explanations. Peter realizes that the best way to make this conversation productive is by showing them the benefit his team's improvement has produced: it has substantially improved response time and reliability of the user application. This changes the tone of the conversation, and Peter's bosses realize this can be reported further upstairs as an achievement, especially because it directly benefits business users, and successes in that area are not particularly frequent. After promising to send them a detailed improvement report, Peter goes back to his teams and provides the exact same update to them, adding: "They are fully onboard with the change we've made, guys. Congratulations on a job well done!"

At the next planning session, Chris and Natalie already have new improvement ideas. Inspired by seeing the two of them succeed, three of their teammates also come up with some improvement ideas. Although only five of Peter's group of 28 are so engaged, more than half of those 28 are seriously curious about the new initiative. Most of them still habitually refrain from sharing their concerns with Peter, but when he speaks to the entire team about something, they listen.

Over the next three quarters, new innovation and improvement tasks are successfully completed by Peter's teams. A few fail but Peter manages to absorb the impact from his bosses, making sure that the team is not impacted in any negative way. Peter got his management's full attention with Natalie's application improvement idea that has added substantial business value despite the small hiccup along the way. Peter's bosses have learned to be a little bit more patient with him and his people because that's the way for them to score in the eyes of their own bosses. More teams are added to Peter's responsibilities as a result of the improved performance of his group. These days a typical one-on-one for Peter is a packed conversation because the teams have gradually learned that sharing with Peter may actually help resolve something.

Example 2. Customer awareness

A marketing department struggles to acquire a larger market share for the company's great new creation. Marketed as a "complete video conferencing solution" and a "one-stop-shop", the product has not seen good traction on the market. The company attributes the problem to low customer awareness and decides to push harder on all available marketing channels, but this has almost no effect, just as before.

In conversation with her boss, an intern who edits marketing text copy wonders what it really means to have a "problem with customer awareness."

Lorie (the intern's manager): "Well, it means that people are unaware that we exist, I suppose. Or maybe they know that we exist but don't know that we have a great product that could help them. That's how I understand it."

Amanda (the intern): "But do we know that for sure? Or could the problem be something else entirely?"

Lorie: "I honestly think we should mind our own business. I think people who suggested we have a customer awareness problem know what they are doing. We should trust their judgment and focus on how to reach out to those potential customers more effectively."

Amanda: "I'm sure people who suggested it had their reasons to do so. But shouldn't we just find out more detail so we can do our job better ... so we can target the right issue?"

Lorie: "Well, here's the issue: we have low customer awareness. That's good enough to act upon it, isn't it?"

The conversation is over and both get on with their day, but Lorie isn't particularly happy with the way she responded to Amanda's genuine curiosity. She feels like she was overly defensive and is now wondering exactly what caused that unproductive stance. "Maybe there's something to it... something that we just would prefer not to hear," she thinks and decides to explore this issue a little bit deeper on her own.

After Lorie discusses the subject with the marketing director, they decide to run a survey in a focus group composed of individuals they previously advertised to. The response is quite interesting: the majority answered that they don't need a "complete video conferencing solution" because they already use some video conferencing tool and have no desire to move away from it.

Lorie means well but doesn't always express it, and as a form of apology, she assigns Amanda to the team exploring better ways of targeting potential customers. Lorie reminds Amanda to listen before giving an opinion on a subject or asking "tricky questions".

The team begins their quest for better messaging and quickly figures out they don't have much knowledge of the product's functionality. After consulting with the product team, a number of product features are selected as a potential basis to develop better messaging. Things show promise until Amanda asks: "How much are these features actually being used? I mean, by the current users?"

There is no answer to that question because the product team never thought of including feature-level user analytics capability. Existing stats only capture information on how often people use the application and for how long, and how many people interact with each other at a time. A micro-release is completed within two weeks, which includes simple analytics to determine how the different product functions are being used. As existing customers apply the update, the feature usage numbers start to come in.

The stats show the most used features are advanced visual collaboration tools that provide real-time interaction, such as virtual whiteboard, index cards, shared spreadsheet, or real-time polls. When some of these users are interviewed in person, they explain that they use other video tools for conference calling itself, and they only use this product for its powerful real-time collaboration features with great functionality that other platforms simply do not have.

The next step is fairly obvious to everyone. A new campaign is created with a radically different message. "Complete solution" is replaced by "High-performance real-time collaboration". The new message is pushed down all available channels, but to everyone's disappointment, it produces no positive change in customer conversions at all.

Lorie is desperate for an explanation and decides to have a chat with Amanda.

Lorie: "I can't wrap my mind around this. Something isn't adding up for me here. How can our users indicate they care so much about 'real-time collaboration' functionality, but when we build a campaign around that key message, nobody cares?"

Amanda: "I agree, we're missing something."

Lorie: "Like what?"

Amanda: "I don't know. But I think we both know who does."

Lorie: "Who? The users, you mean?"

The team organizes an online session with a customer focus group. The current customers are simply asked to describe in as much detail as possible the ways and circumstances in which they use the tool. The most common usage scenarios are to power corporate training, interactive planning sessions, and problem-solving workshops.

A new ad campaign is developed around these key activities enabled by the real-time collaboration functionality and there is a small but immediate increase in customer conversions, which gradually increases.

Over the next six months, customer testimonies appear, followed by case studies, and discussion forums. It seems that the customer community has started to internalize the concept of the tool that helps them with highly interactive online training, planning, and problem-solving. Customers who saw both the older and the newer ads note that even though the new messaging was right on the money, switching from one campaign to another made them confused and more cautious overall. This is the price of pushing the wrong message across all channels at once. And even though everything ultimately worked out quite well, Lorie believes this confusion slowed the uptake for the new campaign and negatively influenced sales in the short term.

Amanda soon leaves the company to enroll in her master's program and Lorie, sorry about her departure, writes a heartfelt recommendation, emphasizing above all Amanda's ability for critical thinking; "A pretty rare skill," as per Lorie's own words.

Example 3. Test automation

After attempting to automate their tests, a software development team is drastically rethinking their approach. What initially happened was that the team had quickly mastered the test automation framework of their choice and built up the desired level of test coverage. Within a couple of weeks, a large number of automated tests had been created. The team learned how to create pretty complicated tests, how to effectively run them, how to diagnose a problem in the code that failed a test, and so forth. But they were learning the wrong thing. They didn't realize they were running themselves into a corner. Things were fine for a while but later some tests started to show up as "red" on the build report even though neither the tests nor the underlying code had changed. Of course, no one trusts a test mechanism that produces false negatives. The developers were particularly disappointed to see their functionality suddenly throw out errors when it was working just fine a day ago. As a result, people lost enthusiasm for automated testing and ended up simply ignoring the error messages and the test suite altogether.

A long time later, the team manages to investigate and find the problem was in the test data. All tests were developed against the system running on a full production data dump on the back end that was downloaded specifically to power the test environment. While some test scenarios involved "read-only" operations, others were also modifying data. Once the data is modified, any subsequent test run will produce different results than expected, thus failing the tests.

To solve the problem the team explores what their counterparts around the globe are doing. Some suggest avoiding complete end-to-end tests that involve databases and instead only test the business logic itself. This is immediately attempted but quickly rejected, as without proper datasets the testing is too shallow and would miss various impactful defects. Others suggest keeping the test data under version control, just like the source code itself. They tried to version-control the original snapshot of the database but the process of restoring the data dump was so painfully slow that it rendered the test suite practically unusable.

Then somebody gets the idea to see what it would take to make just one specific test work. It has become clear that the test doesn't need data from all the tables in the database, so many tables get purged, making the test data about 70% lighter, but still too big to quickly ramp up and tear down when needed. The next question is what exact records are needed across the remaining tables to make just this test scenario work. After a couple of attempts, such a dataset is selected and the rest of the data purged. This time, however, the selected dataset is barely 0.02% of the initial bulk. The idea pops up to have each test manage its own isolated dataset while keeping the dataset minimalistic.

This seems to be a good solution, but hand-picking datasets is a laborious task. It is decided to cut the number of tests in half, leaving less critical tests out. For a while, the test suite is in order again with tests catching errors with no false negatives.

But only for a while.

Ingrid is a senior developer on the team, actively involved in recasting the test suite, and the one who seemed to have made it work encounters a new problem.

Ingrid: "This is unbelievable, what is it this time? Is there a test somewhere that doesn't keep its own data under version control?"

It turns out to be something entirely different. All test data is under version control. The problem is in the database itself. A piece of new functionality has been recently developed that required a change in the database schema. The change is small but sufficient to fail a number of tests.

Jordan (Ingrid's teammate): "So, are we going to go over the entire test suite and check whether the corresponding dataset needs to be updated? That's an unbelievable amount of work. And error-prone as heck!"

Ingrid: "Agreed! We can't keep dealing with this stupid test suite the way it is ..."

Jordan: "So, what are you saying? Abandon it?"

Ingrid: "No, we can't abandon our test suite. If we abandon the tests, we are back to square one with plenty of defects slipping into production."

Jordan: "Okay then. I wonder if we could reduce the number of tests any further?"

Ingrid: "Oh, come on! How much more do you want to strip that thing? There's hardly anything left. But there's a good point in what you said ..."

Jordan: "Which is?"

Ingrid: "We need to minimize the impact of the schema changes on the tests. Slashing tests is a brutal way to do it, but what if we could achieve the same effect without ditching any tests?"

Jordan: "So, right now we have to do as many checks as there are tests ..."

Ingrid: "Correct. And I wonder if we could somehow automate the discovery of affected datasets?"

Jordan: "That seems too fragile to me." He paused for a few moments and continued: "What if we reused them instead? What if a number of tests would use the same dataset? So, if we had a ratio of tests to datasets as 7:1 for example, the effort required to spot a problem after a change in database schema would be seven times smaller. I think we can totally live with that."

Ingrid: "That is interesting. Look at these two test scenarios and their datasets. They are basically 'siblings'. They only have different data records because they were designed independently of one another. But nothing prevents us from killing one of these datasets and pointing its test scenario to the other one."

A couple of months later, they realize the decision to merge test datasets together was the first step in the right direction. They ultimately have had to separate out all the tests that required "read-only" operations and merge them down, as initially intended. But because the "write" tests could modify the data for its "siblings", it was decided to reload the data every time after any such test would run. They later discovered the test execution process could be run in parallel, with each instance executing only a designated "family" of tests that have a shared dataset. With a little bit of tweaking in the build status aggregation, the system can execute at the speed of the biggest test family, which has been ultimately brought down to a little over a minute. False negatives are occurring very infrequently and only for peculiar, isolated reasons, unrelated to the causes the team seemed to have eliminated before. Most importantly, so many things are successfully caught by those tests, protecting the production environment from painful surprises.

Having considered some examples, let's see what truly matters to a successful emergence of a solution, and how it can be vectored towards better outcomes.

Behavior and Its Mental Model

There is something all of our examples have in common. What has to emerge is not just a new behavior but also the apparatus that governs it – a mental model of that behavior.

We act according to our mental model of the world, in the context of a given task. A mental model is a kind of a blueprint of reality which we trust and use to guide our behavior. When weeding our backyard or writing a line of code or making a presentation to investors, we operate according to some model that has developed in our brain. We might not be conscious of the model as it is often implicit or tacit in nature, driving behavior in an unconscious way. A model can be accurate, somewhat accurate, or completely inaccurate in how it represents reality. It would be logical to expect that in order to succeed with a complex task we need to have a proper representation of the world. (Paradoxically though, a wrong mental model is sometimes the only path to producing favorable outcomes. But understanding what mental models govern an individual's behavior remains vitally important. Any change in behavior is anchored in a mental model, whether the model is right or wrong.)

Mental models play a central role in each of the eight examples we considered above. In fact, both the bottleneck and the solution to the bottleneck are dependent upon the underlying mental models of the people involved.

- **Poor discipline in business processes.** As an employee, how should I act? Is it okay to be a little late for work today? Is it okay for me to send out work I haven't checked over? Or on the opposite, maybe I believe I must join the daily planning meeting, rain or shine. And maybe I check work over several times before sending it. An employee's mental model of work discipline is made up of countless similar bits. This deeply embedded mental model is what governs employee behavior, rather than the employee handbook, or job descriptions, or politely worded memos, or policies established by committees. These things will only influence behavior if they get imprinted on the mental model. In a sense, the bottleneck, or the problem, *is* a wrong mental model of the work discipline, and the solution *is* a new and established mental model of how to effectively operate in the enterprise.

- **Distrust of management limiting employee productivity.** If you trust someone, it means you have a mental model that says something like: "I can work with this person, I can share ideas with this person, I can have a difficult conversation with this person and not worry about the consequences of doing so." Unless such a mental model emerges and is sustained over time, there's no trust between you and the other person. Trust cannot be "declared", it can only emerge. The example with Peter and his new group demonstrates this very well.

- **Lack of customer awareness hindering product sales.** Good customer awareness means a customer has an idea in their mind, or a mental model, something like this: "This company has the right product for me, that helps me achieve my objectives, or makes me better at something, or solves some problem that I have" or "They offer a decent product for a very good price" or even "The product is good and their support team is responsive and helpful". Customer awareness depends on some kind of mental anchor in their mind about the brand. A customer's mental model can also encompass a bad perception, either of the company itself or its product. Or the perception can be neutral if the perceived brand isn't relevant to customer goals, as in Lorie and Amanda's marketing efforts.

- **Lack of test automation blocking a software development process.** It might appear that the solution to this bottleneck is just "more tests", but Ingrid and Jordan's experience shows otherwise. The tests themselves are the least complicated component of the solution, and the bigger and much more prominent part is the team's balancing of test coverage and maintainability of the tests. The team had to grow a mental model of how to effectively sustain tests throughout the development process. Naturally, the mental model should be shared across the team members, otherwise conflicting ideas will cause problems in dealing with tests. (Note, however, that a "shared mental model" is not a prerequisite to a good outcome, as it might propagate a systemic error. Also, creativity and innovation thrive on a diversity of mental models.)

- **Poor user experience with IT systems impacting business processes.** A mental model of an IT system grows out of multiple usage scenarios in different specific business contexts, and the same system might be used very differently depending on the particular workflows in the environment. A user's mental model of the software system connects the software capabilities with the scenarios those capabilities support, and with the user goals the scenarios allow them to achieve.

- **Sustained conflict limiting executive team productivity.** Sustained conflict results from an established mental model that the other person is fundamentally wrong, poses a substantial threat or represents an opportunity to expand the sphere of influence. It is deeply rooted in the idea that the only effective way to deal with a particular person is in a confrontational manner. Unless this conviction changes and a new mental model emerges, it is impossible to resolve the conflict.

- **High attrition preventing expertise development.** Why do people leave? While there can be multiple different reasons depending on the organizational context, people have an idea of something being wrong (or not good enough) with their current employment, and an idea they would be better off somewhere else. Retention can only be improved if the employees' mental model regarding their current employment changes compared to the alternatives.

- **Lack of skills limiting team performance.** A skill is acquired gradually through trial and error. A large part of a skill-related mental model can be a mystery, even to its owner. Yet a part of it is conscious and accounts for intentional steps as a part of applying a skill to a task.

The mental model of a complex activity is itself a complex structure consisting of very many elements and relationships, and this is one of the reasons it is so hard to "extract" a *complete* mental model of a particular subject from a person. The other reason lies in how the brain "stores" a mental model. Even though we would like to think of a mental model as a well-structured (preferably hierarchical) system of knowledge stored in one place, in reality, it is spread across a vast number of loosely coupled mental circuits. When a stimulus comes from the environment, the brain knows perfectly well where to route it to in order to get to the right response. But to recover a complete mental model, you would have to take a full inventory of all possible preconditions, which is an immensely hard task.

Here is an example of a complex mental model relating to "Distrust of management limiting employee productivity", which has been purposefully simplified to facilitate understanding, rather than trying to follow how a mental model is really stored in the brain.

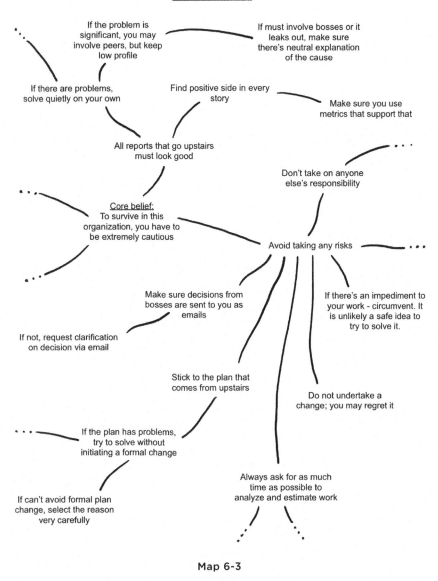

Map 6-3

Here's a mental model of the same subject, only for a different person in a different organization:

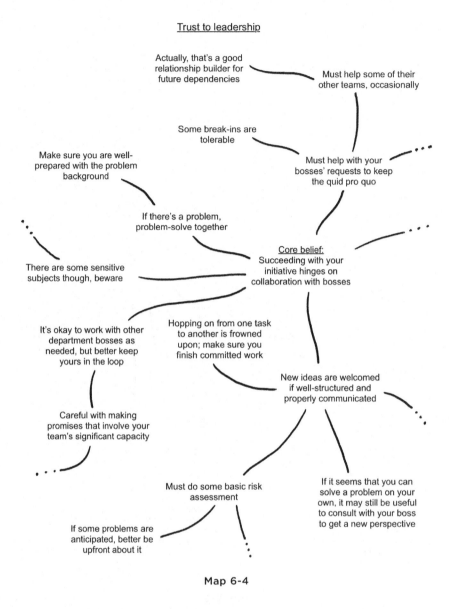

Trust to leadership

Actually, that's a good relationship builder for future dependencies

Must help some of their other teams, occasionally

Some break-ins are tolerable

Make sure you are well-prepared with the problem background

Must help with your bosses' requests to keep the quid pro quo

If there's a problem, problem-solve together

There are some sensitive subjects though, beware

Core belief:
Succeeding with your initiative hinges on collaboration with bosses

It's okay to work with other department bosses as needed, but better keep yours in the loop

Hopping on from one task to another is frowned upon; make sure you finish committed work

New ideas are welcomed if well-structured and properly communicated

Careful with making promises that involve your team's significant capacity

Must do some basic risk assessment

If it seems that you can solve a problem on your own, it may still be useful to consult with your boss to get a new perspective

If some problems are anticipated, better be upfront about it

Map 6-4

The two people have such drastically different mental models about the same subject, encompassing distinctive beliefs, and the behavior governed by these mental models will be very different as well.

The perception of any new signals is affected by the underlying mental model. The mental model acts as a kind of smart filter that sifts out what it considers irrelevant and connects the important bits to core beliefs, thus *constructing the meaning* and preparing the response. If both people, for example, received an email from their supervisor suggesting that the supervisor wants to discuss their current project, the email would be interpreted in radically different ways. The first person might activate the following "pathway":

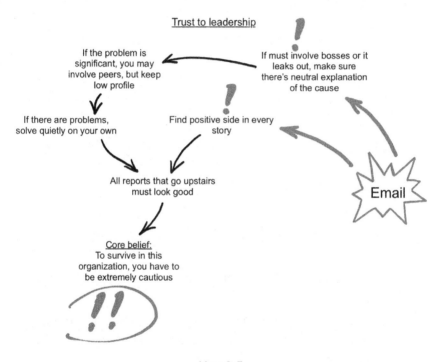

Map 6-5

And the interpretation might be: "Something must be really wrong! Should I clear out my desk?" The second person would navigate to a completely different conclusion:

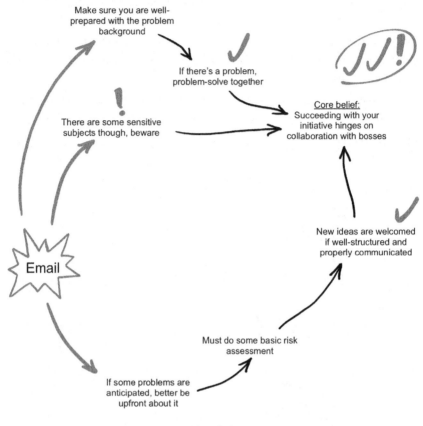

Map 6-6

The second person would be expecting a further improvement in collaboration with their boss and thus further advancement with the task at hand.

Early in the chapter, we considered an example where management required certain behavior from their employees and it didn't work out because the underlying mental models did not evolve towards a more productive behavior. Such "resistance to change" in terms of mental models is extremely common. Core beliefs are often tightly bound to threats or opportunities for success. For the first mental model (Map 6-3), the core belief of "To survive in this organization, you have to be extremely cautious" is directly connected to a threat of losing career opportunities (or even the job itself) if bosses begin to think that there's uncertainty associated with the results of the employee's work. The employee's likely career growth is increased if they keep away from any unnecessary problems or change because both of these things raise the level of uncertainty. In the second case (Map 6-4), the core belief of "Succeeding with your initiative hinges on collaboration with bosses" is tied to an opportunity to grow their career and have fun and a sense of accomplishment at work.

It is fascinating how enterprises build "solutions" that tend to focus on building all the secondary components, while completely ignoring the primary one: the mental model that ultimately governs the behavior of people and is the key to achieving favorable outcomes.

(Note that our simplification, while helpful in demonstrating how diverse mental models produce different behaviors, should be treated very carefully. In reality, the response to a stimulus is not uniquely predetermined but rather potentiated by a large number of adjacent parameters. Because of that, the result of the stimulus is rather one selection out of a broad spectrum of potential responses. Moreover, mental models should not be thought of as static objects; instead, they are pretty fluid and constantly morph as a result of multiple concurrent unconscious processes.)

Emergence Loop

The three examples described earlier in this chapter ("trust to leadership", "customer awareness" and "automated testing") all follow the same pattern of emergence:

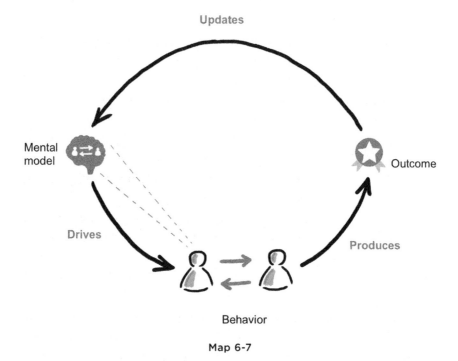

Map 6-7

A mental model drives behavior. In turn, behavior produces certain outcomes, and perception of the outcomes influences the mental model. In the "Automated testing" example, the team's initial mental model was "More tests = higher chances of catching errors" and they created as broad a test coverage as reasonably possible. When such a test suite proved to be unsustainable because of the lack of control over the test database, their mental model was updated to "Test data must be version-controlled".

Acting with this mental model solved the problem with volatile data but the new problem of severely fragmented test data was introduced, creating a serious problem every time the database schema was updated. The team's mental model evolved to "Similar datasets have to be merged to minimize repercussions of a schema update".

Overall, the emergence of a solution can be thought of as an upward spiral process:

Emergent solution

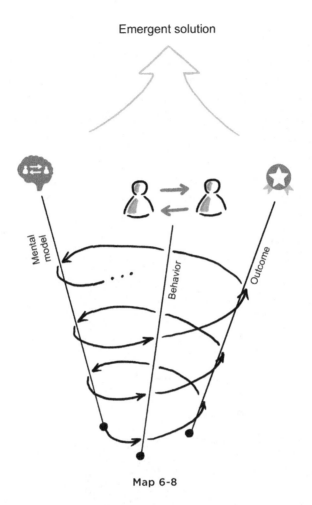

Map 6-8

It is crucial to keep in mind that the loop exists whether we realize it or not. Human behavior develops in a loop like this, along with our mental models. This is the way we evolved to operate and there's no escaping this fundamental pattern. The only thing in question is whether it will be the loop we want or a loop that will produce undesired results.

The emergence loop does not exist in a vacuum. Mental models and their corresponding behaviors are subject to the influence of environmental factors. This is a crucial way to tap into the cycle and vector the emergence in a favorable direction.

Solution Trajectory, Enablers and Constraints

Our goal is to influence the emergence loop so that we arrive at a really good solution. It is important to remind ourselves that neither mental models nor behaviors can be "constructed". But the process of emergence can still be influenced by introducing proper *enablers* and *constraints*.

Enablers and constraints are extremely dependent on context. A software system is an enabler for its users. It can actually be a constraint, too. So can a policy, an action of a leader, a change in the structure of the organization, a new incentive model, a test suite, a marketing campaign, and so on. Enablers and constraints act as moderators of the emergence process.

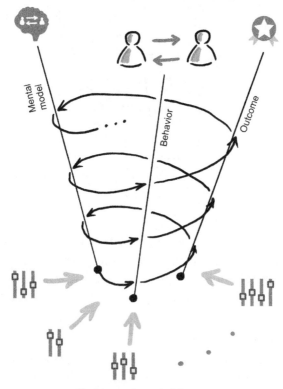

Enablers and constraints

Map 6-9

The primary purpose of enablers and constraints is to activate the emergence loop, so the solution can emerge over multiple cycles. Enablers and constraints are not the solution. Mental models, behaviors, and outcomes that formed under the influence of enablers and constraints, constitute the solution.

Nobody cares about software that cannot induce productive user behavior. Nobody cares about a new organizational incentive program, with all its beautiful PowerPoint slides and corporate web portal support, if people continue to leave the company in search of a better career. Nobody cares about a thorough skill training program if the employees are still helpless in dealing with professional challenges that arise in their workplace.

Depending on what enablers and constraints are applied and how they are applied, the "trajectory" of solution emergence may take different shapes. The idea is to prevent the solution from evolving towards unfavorable outcomes.

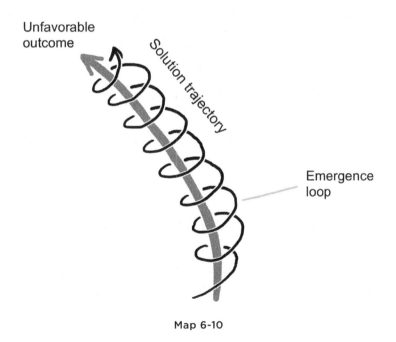

Map 6-10

Instead, effectively applying enablers and constraints should guide the solution trajectory toward outcomes that would provide substantial benefit.

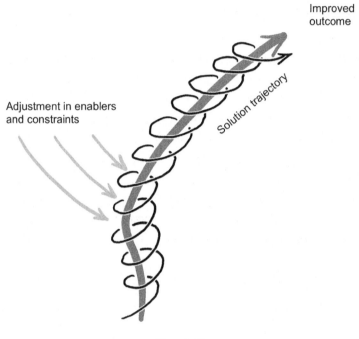

Map 6-11

If used correctly, enablers and constraints are the "control mechanism" that guides solutions in a productive direction.

Qualitative Shifts and Adaptations

Emergence is a radically different process than design. One of the core characteristics is that emergence cannot be planned up-front. An attempt to plan emergence leads to failure as the ecosystem will "respond" by producing pathological behaviors that are a lot harder to fix. All three examples show that what ultimately works out can be quite different from the originally intended idea of a behavior.

Every "coil" of emergence loop designates one of the two fundamental processes: a qualitative shift or an adaptation. And the evolution of the system behavior as a whole can be thought of as:

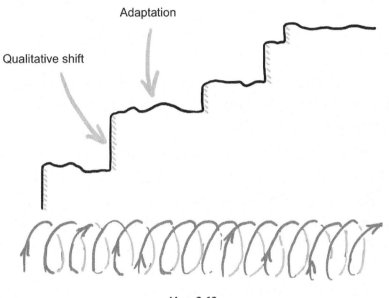

Map 6-12

System behavior evolves as a result of qualitative shifts followed by a series of adaptations.

A qualitative shift results in novel aspects of behavior but also a leap in the mental model of behavior. New realizations emerge that weren't available just one cycle back. In fact, some aspects of the new mental model would likely appear illogical or even ridiculous just a cycle before.

If somebody had told Ingrid and her team in the "Test automation" example that they would end up manually composing test datasets that would be shared across a certain number of test scenarios and keeping them under version control system, they would have laughed at the idea, and yet their solution trajectory ultimately led them to this realization, and once they got there, it all appeared completely natural and logical.

Similarly, if someone told Peter in the "Trust with leadership" example that trust would grow out of confrontation and that his team's failure to clearly formulate the tasks would end up solidifying a productive relationship, he wouldn't be likely to take it too seriously either.

In other words, the process of emergence is inherently asymmetrical:

The evolution of a mental model of emergent behavior appears perfectly reasonable retrospectively but completely unreasonable prospectively.

This asymmetry can, and should, be leveraged. Essentially this means:

Qualitative shifts cannot be predicted, but when they are about to take place (or just took place), they can be recognized and taken advantage of.

While it is virtually impossible to predict the evolution of a complex system, it is relatively easy to recognize the utility of a certain development once it is already in place, even if it was entirely unintended. Chris and Natalie were initially unhappy with Peter requiring additional detail on the task goals, but ultimately they found the interaction with him inspiring and comforting. Similarly, Peter later recognized the product of that extra effort was useful to communicate the task benefits to his bosses, even though that was not in his original plan.

You have to embrace uncertainty in order to help facilitate the successful emergence of a complex solution. While the agent of a system may not have predictive power over certain opportunities, they may be able to recognize an opportunity when it presents itself. This is why the next mental model cannot be explained from the perspective of the previous one: it has features the previous one didn't have and couldn't have, as they were not created intentionally but recognized once they presented themselves in an unexpected way.

Strategies for Emergence of Effective Solutions
Preserving flexibility

One of the core characteristics of an emergent process is that it holds significant unknowns. Making premature choices or committing to a certain course of action early on will incur significant cost later. In our previous examples we've seen this happening. The original approach to creating tests did not work out and required quite a bit of rework. In the case with customer awareness, the company was fully committed to a vast marketing campaign based on the wrong message. Besides money wasted on a wrong campaign, even after the company found the right messaging, the change caused confusion among customers and slowed down sales early on. The teams were able to find the right solution eventually, in both of these examples, but getting there might have been unnecessarily expensive.

Committing to a certain choice prematurely is not a good idea while preserving flexibility enables much better outcomes. Here are some ways to enable flexibility:

Only make the required decisions. Consider using the following two simple categories for decisions: urgent and non-urgent. The first step is to categorize according to this simplistic model. Urgent decisions need to be made, so that becomes the first order of business. But non-urgent decisions are where lots of the benefit can be gained by *not* making them early. When postponed, they allow for the critical bit of information to transpire, and only then can those decisions be made in an informed way.

If we can gain so much by postponing less urgent decisions, how much do we lose when we make urgent decisions early? Just because a decision is urgent does not imply that we have enough information to make a good call. There's a likelihood of losing something on urgent decisions, but there's a reason why they are urgent. Avoiding making these decisions in the near term would be detrimental to the outcome. More to the point, does the cost of not making an urgent decision in time outweigh the cost of making it early when there's little information? The question obviously is contextual and we are talking about very fuzzy variables. How can anyone reliably know the impact of unknowns beforehand? The best you can do is roughly assess your level of knowledge about something, even though that might be unreliable due to cognitive bias favoring an overly optimistic view of reality.

A few things can be done:

- Assess the amount of uncertainty in a decision, to the best of your knowledge. Involving others, especially people of different roles and backgrounds, will mitigate cognitive bias.

- Use proactive hindsight (pre-mortem) on such decisions. The process is described in detail in Chapter 4.

- Consider splitting urgent decisions that contain a high degree of uncertainty or too many problems. "Splitting" a decision means carving out a part of it and only committing to that part for now, while postponing the rest until later. The split will result in a more urgent part and a less urgent part. We will go into this technique in more detail later in the chapter when talking about vertical slicing.

In the automated test example, instead of committing to creating a large number of tests in the test framework of choice, the decision could be split into two parts:

Part 1: Select test framework and design first 20 tests

Part 2: Create desired test coverage for the whole system

A lot of effort lies in Part 2, and that is clearly where the team would benefit from making an informed decision, but Part 1 is extremely likely to reveal that information. Executing Part 1 first, and then Part 2 after a while, could be very beneficial.

How long should a delay between the two parts be? It's more useful to ask whether anything has been learned since Part 1 was executed, and therefore more reasonable to think of the delay in terms of emergence cycles rather than days, weeks, or months. Cycling through the loop a few times with the initial 20 tests and all the way to the outcome (i.e. "being able to catch defects") would have a high likelihood of revealing the problem, allowing adjustments to be made to the initial 20 tests, and some new tests added.

Map 6-13

Maintain multiple options. The method assumes sustaining different variants of the solution at the same time until there's sufficient information to support a choice of one over the other. In the customer awareness example, two marketing campaigns could have been maintained with two (or more) different types of messaging behind them. This is an example of *explicit* options.

Solution options can also be maintained *implicitly* when it is not the options themselves being maintained, but rather their potentiality. In the case of our marketing campaign, some signals appear suggesting that the company's online collaboration tools are mostly used by technical people who require a lot of real-time diagramming, but because the team is not entirely convinced of the validity of this evidence, they only nudge the messaging in that direction, but not in a way that would cut off the rest of potential user categories. Instead of going with something like "Plan your product design and implementation together!" they continue on with a more careful message: "Create diagrams, figures, and charts together!" The difference is important because you will be eager to license the tool whether you are a software developer, or a hardware engineer, a financial advisor, a sales representative, a marketing professional, and so on.

Explicit and implicit options have their pros and cons.

Explicit options are good because all options are real, tangible, and provoke the environment to reveal its workings as the solution is actually progressing down multiple trajectories. The flip side of that is the cost of maintaining multiple actual options.

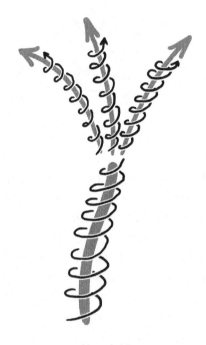

Map 6-14

Using the approach hinges on reaching a balance between the cost of maintaining multiple options and the learning facilitated by the options, ultimately allowing the best option to be selected.

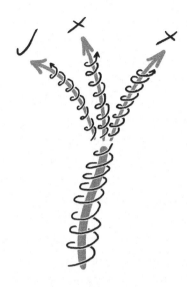

Map 6-15

Implicit options are good because they come at no direct cost. There is only one solution option at a time, but it preserves the flexibility to evolve in different directions if needed.

Map 6-16

Implicit options are incredibly useful when there are multiple parameters in question. One parameter might be that you are not sure what profession to market your product to, but others might be multiple geographies, age groups, proficiency levels, cultures, and so on. Different variations with multiple parameters quickly add up into huge numbers of solution options and maintaining them as implicit, potential variants (rather than real ones) is the only feasible way to preserve flexibility. On the other hand, "potentiality" does not equal "reality". Sometimes we rely too much on our judgment of the viability of those options. The real test would be actually implementing them. Also, while preserving implicit options does not incur any direct cost (because there is only one tangible option at any time), there is an implicit cost that can sometimes be pretty significant. Trying to preserve potential options may actually constrain the solution in its ability to pursue any particular option far enough. In our marketing example, it is possible the message of "Create diagrams, figures and charts together!" may not actually resonate well with any audience, even though it is pretty inclusive of all potential customer categories.

For multiple options to work effectively, selective pressure is required. A strong, fast, and reliable feedback loop helps to distinguish between options and select what works better. Without selective pressure, the effort is largely futile as the options that "win" may have nothing to do with the actual viability of the solution.

Ascend the outcome chain. Immediate outcomes are only stepping stones to the ultimate outcome on the outcome chain. There can be alternative pathways to the ultimate outcome. We saw this outcome chain in Chapter 4:

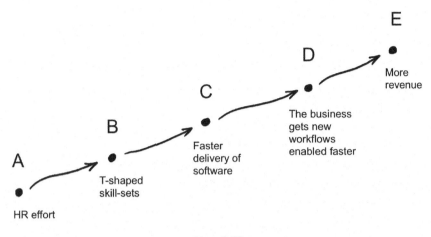

Map 6-17

Instead of trying to stick to the originally envisioned outcome chain above, the organization discovered that a different approach would be more effective in achieving higher-order outcomes:

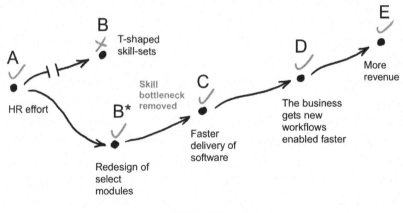

Map 6-18

This is what ascending the outcome chain is: placing primary emphasis on higher-order outcomes and considering lower-level outcomes only as means to an end. And if there are better alternatives at the lower-level, they should be pursued to deliver ultimate benefit to the organization.

To ascend the outcome chain:

1 Identify the outcome chain

2 Define alternatives to the immediate outcome on the chain

3 Evaluate alternatives based on how well they enable higher-order outcomes.

Ascending the outcome chain is an extension to the concept of preserving multiple options considered above, but we are not limiting ourselves by a certain immediate outcome. In Map 6-18, solution alternatives were assessed based on the second-order outcome, at node B. Sometimes ascension can go past second-order and into higher-order outcomes. The further you ascend, the broader the landscape of solution alternatives opens up.

Activating the Emergence Loop Early

A common scenario of failure among organizations is to determine the bottleneck (trust, psychological safety, discipline, skill-sets) and then design the solution. When the solution is delivered months later, it fails to do what it was supposed to do. The solution was built based on numerous assumptions, layered on top of each other. Paradoxically, this may be done "in pursuit of predictability" and is often encouraged by the chain of command as having a plan offers everyone a strongly comforting feeling that the initiative is "under control". But the probability of the whole chain of assumptions to work out as expected equals zero! Just because somebody wants certainty doesn't mean it can be achieved with more speculation. Meaningful exposure of the solution to its ecosystem early in the process could have revealed the problems and prevented failure.

But that is easier said than done!

For us to obtain sensible feedback, the part of the solution exposed earlier has to "stir up" impactful scenarios in the ecosystem, activating the emergence loop, and connecting mental models, behaviors, and outcomes into a meaningful cycle.

A *"horizontal"* slice of the ecosystem is something organizations opt for almost by default, spending a lot of time creating software systems, employee training courses, policies, campaigns, guidelines, only to be exposed to the rest of the ecosystem after all the work is finished:

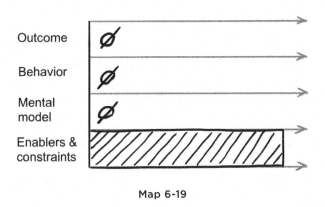

Map 6-19

Instead of that horizontal slice, we need to perform a *"vertical"* slice of the ecosystem:

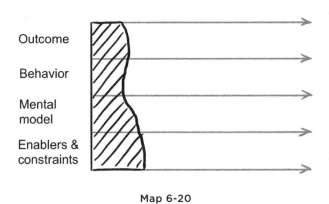

Map 6-20

Here are some examples of horizontal and vertical slices for the areas introduced earlier in the chapter:

- **Lack of skills limiting team performance.** A *horizontal* slice would be thoroughly training employees in new skills and only then letting them leverage the knowledge, which works much better on the slides of corporate presentations than in reality. A much more intelligent approach would be to abandon the idea of a skill as a monolith and instead view it as a collection of smaller components, just as we looked at a complex asset where each skill would deliver value over different value paths. A subset of those paths could be selected as a first *vertical* slice over the skill. If the skill in question is graphic design for a marketing campaign, a slice of it could be based on non-vector graphics. Or it could be basic work with layers. Or something else that allows the person to complete some basic tasks that can produce results. The skill is acquired only if the person can apply it to deliver something of value. And with any such vertical slice, we are activating the emergence loop as early as possible, by letting the person apply the skill to produce a meaningful outcome.

- **Poor discipline in business processes.** Our idea of a solution might be to increase the visibility of the results of work by shortening the accountability cycle, utilizing team objectives with daily planning and closure routines. New standards of output quality and productivity are expected to come out of this. A *horizontal* slice would be to create detailed presentations of the new process, familiarize facilitators and team leads with it, and establish the process with their teams. Such a "big bang" approach would require phenomenal luck to actually succeed. A *vertical* slice would implement the method in just a few teams, instead of the entire organization. Success would mean that not only the "enablers and constraints" were delivered but also that the mental model and actual behavior changed, and produced a distinct outcome. If it turns out that people have become eager to use the rapid planning-execution cycle, and really care about their task completion during the day, and create peer pressure for closing the day with a quick review of results, then we know that we are moving in the right direction.

- **Distrust of management limiting employee productivity.** We can look back at how Peter started rebuilding trust with the teams he was assigned to. He picked one particular area of concern (improvement items) and a few people who showed some desire to take on improvement opportunities, and he activated the emergence loop on this small subset. As a result, more people got engaged in improvement activities, creating more impact.

- **Lack of customer awareness hindering product sales.** A *horizontal* approach would be building a full-blown campaign and pushing it down all channels. A *vertical* approach might run one particular message on a subset of potential customers. The transition from costly horizontal to much more productive vertical slicing is what happened with Lorie and her team.

- **Lack of test automation blocking a software development process.** Going with all tests at once was Ingrid and Jordan's early mistake: a perfect example of a *horizontal* slice. They would have been more productive if they had created coverage for some portion of the functionality that was expected to undergo change. This would have activated the full loop much faster and led them to the ultimate solution more productively. Covering only a portion of the software system's functionality with tests is a *vertical* slice in this case.

- **Poor user experience with IT systems impacting business processes.** A *horizontal* way is to deliver both software and customer training and then wish your corporate users good luck. A more productive *vertical* slice would be a subset of the functionality and a corresponding subset of the training, possibly delivered to a fraction of the entire user base, which will tell us if the development effort for the software itself goes in the right direction.

There is a huge similarity between the way we created vertical slices and the way probing scenarios were designed in Chapter 4, because they are essentially equivalent activities, and *vertical slicing is a form of direct probing* of the environment.

The early activation of the emergence loop has profound impacts, allowing us to see whether the system is moving in the right direction, and take corrective action if it is not.

The early activation of the emergence loop can reveal, for instance, that the enablement system is incomplete. Looking back at "Lack of skills limiting team performance", let's say that instead of running comprehensive training on "Network Administration" we went with a small module on "Managing Ports". The training module should introduce some basic mental models sufficient to start working with ports. The people who just went through the training module would pick some actual tasks to open, close, and monitor ports. It soon turns out, however, that port monitoring is the only one of the three tasks they advanced on. The problem with the other tasks wasn't actually knowledge related, because the network admins already learned from the training module how to open or close a port. They were just overcautious in performing any of these operations because they lacked a good knowledge of what impact opening or closing a port would have on their organization's network. Fear of causing data loss, or exposing the organization to potential cyberthreats prevented progress down the loop. More enablement was needed to successfully fulfill the task. Once they had a basic idea of what else was hooked up to the network and got introduced to other teams responsible for maintaining key applications in the network, they started advancing on their main tasks. At this point, the process of growing the skill has effectively begun.

Understanding the Underlying Motivations

The motivation of people who are a part of a solution is vital to putting the emergence loop into motion, but the *actual* motivation of individuals in the system is often very different from what is *expected* to drive their behavior. As a matter of fact, organizational purpose and the individual motivations of people comprising the organization are always different.

But how can anything be achieved in an enterprise or a team with this divergence?

The answer is quite simple: even divergent motivation can be leveraged to produce beneficial outcomes. Here are some examples.

1   Skill. The organization wants to have high-skilled employees so the workforce can be leveraged more productively. Employees might also want to improve skill-sets, but to a potentially different reason: to grow their career faster, or even to find a better job somewhere else. This motivation can still be leveraged to improve the performance of the teams.

2   Quality. The organization wants to deliver a quality product and customers want a high-quality product, but for different reasons. The organization needs a certain level of quality to win over the competition and avoid negative customer reviews or even lawsuits. The customers want a quality product for its improved utility or status or some other way it benefits them.

3   Conflict. The company needs employees to stay out of the unproductive conflict because conflict can cause productivity to go down. Conflict might even translate into liability issues on the part of the organization. Employees, on the other hand, want to stay out of the unproductive conflict because of the emotional cost.

But divergent motivation cannot always be leveraged. Sometimes the divergence is too significant for the system to be productive. Perhaps an organization wants its employees to work extra time while the employees do not want to, or the company might want customers to buy a product suite while the majority of customers only want a single product to satisfy a specific need, which allows them to save money.

The way the solution emerges can be heavily impacted by this divergence in motivation whether the ultimate result is beneficial or not.

This is how the solution might emerge in undesired ways:

1   Skill. While both the organization and the employees desire skill development, the skills that help with career might be developed more than skills the organization needs. This might lead to a serious shortage in some skill areas, or influence the depth of skills. The higher-order outcome of having a better organizational performance might not be achieved to the desired extent or end up completely botched due to this mismatch.

2   Quality. The organization might only focus on the aspects of quality that give them leverage over its competition or keeps them out of trouble in terms of liability, but this doesn't necessarily benefit the consumer. The product might be safe to use and fewer defects are reported by customers, but they are still experiencing usability issues. The company, however, doesn't bother spending time and money to improve usability simply because competitors also have poor product usability, and it is not believed by the company management that improved UX would offer any economic leverage.

3   Conflict. Drained by excessive confrontation, employees may avoid conflict by avoiding collaboration. The company wanted to reduce conflict, but this natural—yet unfortunate—solution will only increase disconnects and end up producing worse results for the business.

The higher-order outcomes must be kept in mind to keep the system moving in the right direction, but might not be enough to succeed with the task. Some work needs to be done to nudge the process of emergence down a beneficial trajectory, and that requires some changes on the part of enablers and constraints. Here are some examples:

1   Skill. The organization could look into why people prefer certain skill areas over others in terms of career growth and discover that improving career choices, recognition, compensation, and so on, would encourage people to stay with the company after learning new skills.

COMPLEX BOTTLENECKS AND EMERGENT SOLUTIONS

2 Quality. The organization might look at some higher-order outcomes as well as the immediate ones, but sometimes that creates an overly narrow view, limiting the perspective to only what's desired rather than what may really happen. Instead, looking into collateral outcomes might reveal a lot of missing information. Improved UX might grant significant benefits in the form of increased customer loyalty and the desire to purchase other products. This wouldn't be considered within the narrow perspective of quarterly sales goals for existing products.

3 Conflict. Instead of just demanding less unproductive conflict, the organization might actually help teams get through conflict in a constructive way with the help of team leaders or facilitators, offering a glimmer of hope for future collaboration.

Overcoming Resistance to Change

The emergence of a solution is commonly hindered by the current state of equilibrium. It can become incredibly hard to create momentum in any direction that would take the system out of its current sweet spot. Wherever the problem manifests, it has one universal characteristic: resistance to change. Given that a complex solution always involves a certain change in human behavior, these key points characterize the problem:

1 A person does not believe a certain action will produce a favorable outcome

2 Should they have performed the anticipated action, it would have become clear that the action was beneficial

3 But they will not do that because of "1"

The reasons for resistance to change are understandable. Any state of equilibrium for a social system becomes deeply ingrained in the context of the system. The equilibrium behavior becomes pretty efficient over the course of multiple adaptations, so any deviation from it appears to lead to a worse outcome.

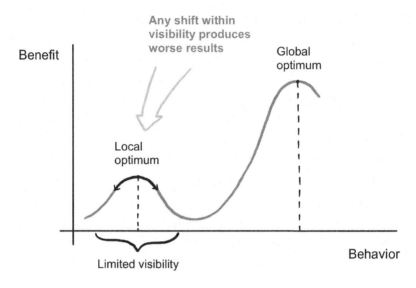

Map 6-21

But limited visibility prevents the system from seeing beyond their local optimum, and the better solution that exists beyond the span of visibility remains a missed opportunity, either not noticed, or seen as irrelevant.

This is a stalemate situation for many organizations. A lack of psychological safety holds people back from "giving it a shot". But if they feel unsafe about trying (and possibly failing) then they most certainly will feel unsafe reporting that they are not acting according to the expectation.

Resistance to change was highlighted in the example where nobody on Peter's team had any desire to engage in any activities that would require trust in leadership.

Resistance means that the emergence loop will never be directed towards a behavior substantially different than the current one. And if proper emergence loop is never entered, the solution will have no chance to grow into a viable state, so solving this problem is extremely important.

Peter did a couple of interesting things in the example. First, he explored what was behind the profound lack of trust. Once he learned the group had failed before and certain people had been thrown under the bus when something went wrong, he addressed the issue at its core, by apologizing for those mishaps and sending a clear message that the underlying problem was recognized. He built on that foundation by finding people who would be eager to try something new and achieve a good result. He worked with them directly, paying a lot of attention to how the initial effort went. He used every opportunity to remove obstacles to their success. Once the first few people started to manifest new behavior, others could see from the example of their peers that trust was actually possible to establish, and might also propel you towards your goals. In time, others joined in.

To overcome resistance to change we need to understand that people don't know what they don't know. Novel behavior produces an effect they cannot currently comprehend, due to the knowledge asymmetry we discussed earlier. The idea of moving toward the new behavior involves reservations, and possibly even fear. If they could magically hop over the chasm between their current mental model and the future one, there would be no problem. But that essentially defines the following main possibilities:

1   Invite them to perform the action even if its meaning will only be clear later. This may require negotiation and trust, but other fundamental drivers, like curiosity, desire to improve, might be instrumental and should be used to help the group overcome the gap in understanding.

2   Give them a sense of what it feels like to be on the other side. If someone has already "crossed the chasm", they can become a "proxy" for the new mental model. This is not as profound as learning from your own experience, but it can have quite a powerful effect.

Extracting the Context

Growing a successful solution hinges on establishing a productive emergence loop that connects mental models, behavior, and outcomes for the people involved. But what are the *current* mental models, *current* behaviors, and *current* outcomes they achieve with their current behavior and thought process?

The easiest, and most profoundly wrong, shortcut is to make some assumptions about the three components of the loop. Organizations often assume they know what their customers or users or employees or partners want, do, or achieve. A lot of effort might be spent on building something based on such assumptions, and this is why so many enterprise initiatives fail. Emergence loop has an incredibly deep and complex context that must be uncovered, not assumed.

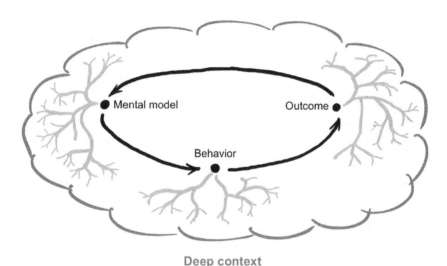

Deep context

Map 6-22

Recovering this context is not a trivial task, but it can benefit from probing the environment. Let's look in more detail at how to recover valuable context with each component of the emergence cycle.

Mental model. It is impossible to "download" someone's mental model, mainly—as it has been mentioned before—because there is no single "folder" in our brain where all the information regarding a particular model would be kept. Instead, the information is spread across various circuits, each responding to a certain set of preconditions, a scenario of sorts. So, one part of the challenge of recovering a mental model comes from the difficulty of taking inventory of all scenarios. This is the *breadth* problem. Here is an example of the breadth problem. When asked about their take on "work discipline", an employee might mention the importance of showing up at work on time because they have early morning meetings that day. At the same time, they might forget to mention the importance of commitment, staying on task, finishing rather than starting work, and helping each other deal with problems, mainly because those scenarios are not active at the moment, and the brain finds it difficult to navigate to a response without a stimulus. The second challenge is the challenge of *depth*. It might seem that a portion of a mental model has been recovered, but in fact, most of the important details remain hidden. This happens often because *emotion* is an integral part of human cognition, so for some circuits to activate, a person needs to "care enough". *Bias* poses another challenge, as what is believed by an individual to be the case might not necessarily be so in reality. *Intentional error* is yet another challenge, where people don't share the aspects of their mental models they don't feel comfortable revealing. We encountered this in the example with Peter's team members feeling unsafe sharing problems with him early on. Lastly, many aspects of a mental model can be hard to recover because of its *tacitness*. An accountant might be proficient with the use of the IT systems required for their work but most of that knowledge is not fully conscious, instead, residing in the realm of "muscle memory". It might be very difficult for this person to explain how they do what they do, but they could show it. Perhaps they can't even conceptualize it, and unveiling their mental model could be as much of a surprise for them as for the facilitator.

When trying to discover a person's mental model regarding certain context, keep these considerations in mind:

1   Create as much overlap with the person as possible. It's helpful to "spend time with your customer" because you increase your exposure to their mental model of reality. Similarly, when two engineers pair up on a number of tasks, the mental models related to some sophisticated skill or expertise are conveyed much better than by formal training. Always seek more substantial overlap and exposure. An interview is better than a survey. And a close, longer-term interaction is better than any interview.

2   Utilize decision-making venues to explore mental models. Decisions are good markers of the underlying mental models, so tapping into the decision-making process reveals a lot. Some ideas for such venues include budget and effort planning meetings, synchronization and progress status meetings, problem-solving, and reviews.

3   Do not explore mental models in isolation from the rest of the emergence loop. In some sense, the action (behavior) is the best manifestation of a mental model, and the perceived outcome is what influences mental models quite significantly.

Behavior. Asking about behavior and observing it are two very different things. People often provide extremely inaccurate accounts of their own behavior because of bias, emotional impact, and so on. Observation, on the other hand, might provide a deep and unbiased source of insight. But behavior might not be easy to observe. Some types of behavior are self-evident and always stay on the surface, while others are deeply hidden under a layer of "noise". Even within a given context, some aspects of behavior can be quite obvious while others remain completely hidden, and the hidden ones might account for a significant part of the outcome. Customer behavior on the company's e-commerce website may be well captured by the analytics system, and therefore well known. But the reason why customer loyalty is decreasing could be due to a user experience they receive elsewhere, with other vendors, which is well beyond the visibility of the analytics system provided by the company. A lot of actual employee behavior is not truly known but has a big impact on the outcome of their effort. Working towards establishing improved visibility into various aspects of behavior is important.

Things that might improve the ability to see the behavior of a person:

1   Observe. Quite a few customers find it totally acceptable to let you observe their action, knowing this might improve the value proposition.

2   Create analytics instrumentation where possible.

3   Ask people to provide their own account of their behavior. At the same time ask them to provide an account of the actions of others. Compare the notes.

4   Have patience. Certain behavior patterns manifest themselves over significant timeframes.

Outcome. Sometimes the outcome is fairly straightforward and easy to ensure, while sometimes it is intangible and hard to put your finger on. Determining what indicators can be used to ensure achievement of an outcome, is a highly contextual task. But it's a very necessary task, too.

Peter knew that he is on the right track in terms of achieving the outcome of establishing trust with his new teams when after a while he started to see more people coming up with improvement ideas. For Lorie and Amanda, a good sign that their marketing campaign is on the right track was customer conversions. For Ingrid and Jordan, sustained ability to catch defects in development would serve as an indication of successful outcome achievement.

What complicates the matter is that assessing achievement of an outcome often requires human judgment, and as such, it is subjected to unconscious bias. Also, depending on the nature of the environment, outcome indicators can be gamed to show to the management that everything progresses according to a plan. It is very helpful to establish additional controls by examining the connection such indicators have with the higher-order outcomes.

Repairing the Emergence Loop

Quite often the emergence loop itself is a part of the problem. Problems can manifest as disconnects in different parts of the loop.

Broken outcome feedback is where the results of action do not register in the mental model, effectively creating an open-loop system.

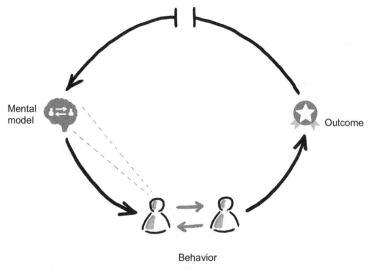

Map 6-23

This can happen because the outcome of the action is simply assumed, but never checked. Some outcomes are self-evident but some require discovery either because they are delayed, or because they manifest in subtle ways. In the testing example, the team did not bother to establish a viable feedback loop for the efficacy of their newly developed tests. They were lucky to discover the problem by accident, but luck is an unreliable method.

A "surrogate" feedback loop can sometimes override the actual one.

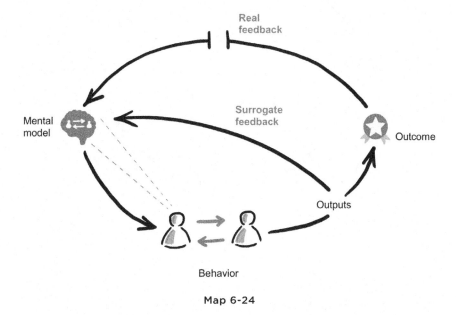

Map 6-24

In the example with test automation, the surrogate feedback was that "all tests are executing correctly". That is not the same as "the tests support the development process by catching defects". The surrogate feedback biased the system and facilitated the growth of the wrong mental model and behavior.

The only viable way to fight this problem is to repair the disconnect in the actual outcome feedback. Exploring outcomes and establishing empirical outcome measures is a good first step. Also, various probing techniques will help reveal which direction the system is moving.

Disconnected action occurs when the idea of a behavior differs systemically from the behavior itself.

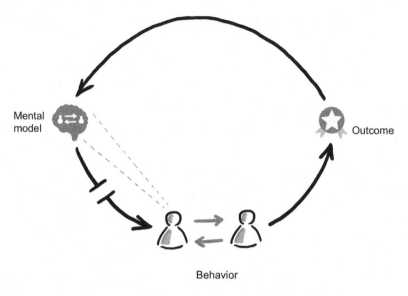

Mental model

Outcome

Behavior

Map 6-25

This is rarely a problem on its own and is often coupled with the previous disconnect, creating a double error: action that doesn't correspond with the mental model appears to "work out" quite well when the outcome feedback is broken. A team of software developers may believe the results of their work are outstanding due to the team's great technical judgment and attention to quality. The other team that receives their outputs, however, has to implement a fair amount of fixes before the software is ready to deploy. They prefer to not deal with this team because of some unfavorable collaboration experiences in the past, and they would rather just fix the issues themselves than ask the team to fix them. As a result of this broken relationship, the other team acts differently than they think they act but also doesn't have a chance to learn that they are not succeeding. Unconscious behavior, cognitive bias, and communication problems are typical contributors to this problem.

Creating Sustainability

A new behavior—even if it has been experienced—doesn't necessarily become a sustained way of operating. In fact, getting to early manifestations of a new behavior sometimes is not all that hard. What is hard is to stabilize the behavior, making it a habit for the people involved.

Integrating a new behavior into an existing ecosystem takes time. A new behavior does not instantly get exposed to the whole set of possible scenarios: this happens gradually. Every time a new such scenario is activated, it puts "pressure" on the new behavior. Ultimately, the pressure may be too strong for the behavior to sustain, and it gives. Here is an example based on "Sustained conflict limiting executive team productivity".

The company invited consultants who conducted a number of sessions with executives, helping them bond better as a team, sparking empathy toward each other, and giving initial momentum toward collaboration. Everybody felt better about it, especially the company CEO who struggled because of his entirely dysfunctional team. The next executive meeting went a lot better. People were much more open-minded than before and seemed ready to listen to each other. The CEO couldn't be happier. He was certain the organization's strategic shift to a new product line would now go a lot smoother.

But it did not.

The first problem occurred when Bryan, the company's marketing executive, was asked to share some of his web developers with Cathrine, the CIO. They had a long-going problem stemming from Cathrine's belief that all developers should be a part of the IT organization, while Bryan maintained that he needed to keep some web developers in his department for fast turn-around on tasks related to marketing. Bryan naturally feared that Cathrine could use the opportunity to simply "appropriate" whoever is given to her to help with IT tasks and never give them back. The problem started to create some difficulties in the interaction between the two groups.

A couple of weeks later, Eugene, the company's Chief Security Officer, initiated a program to recast the underlying communication and authentication protocols to enable an easier transition toward the new product line. The transition would benefit the new set of company products, as well as grant much more flexibility in the future. But Eugene always relied on Cathrine's people for the actual implementation of his ideas, as he only had a small team, mainly security experts who acted as guides to the IT organization. So Eugene liked the idea of moving some people from Marketing to IT. In one of the staff meetings he openly mentioned how much he appreciates the idea of helping each other with people in times of need. In the meantime, the transition to a new security model caused some interruptions in the work of the CRM system. Kelly, Head of Sales, used the opportunity to slam both Security and IT for letting these problems happen, thus giving her long-time ally Bryan the upper hand. From this moment on there was no more empathy and love. The executive team reverted to their habitual equilibrium state.

Here is what happened with the executive team:

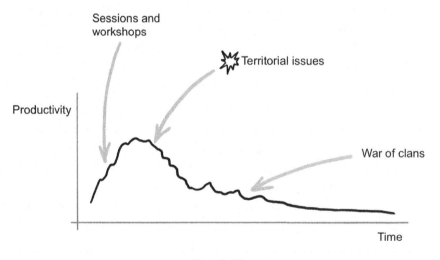

Map 6-26

The spike of early excitement and enthusiasm was interrupted by a problem. The problem was not addressed properly, and a decline followed. In the end, there is no hint to suggest there was ever a period of improved collaboration or improved team productivity.

In contrast, this is what happened in the test automation example:

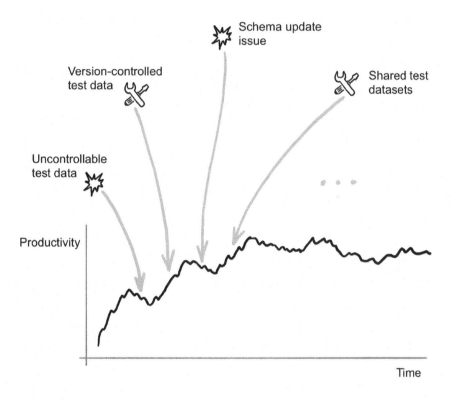

Map 6-27

Every problem was actively worked on by the team. They addressed each issue in turn and didn't let the newly acquired behaviors stall or deteriorate. Once they got past a certain point, test automation became a team habit.

To get from a newly acquired behavior to a habit, impediments must be actively and continuously addressed.

At the point where a *habit* is formed, the shape of the behavior can be quite different from what was initially manifested, and even more different than the way it was originally intended. This is another example of the asymmetry of the emergence process, as discussed earlier in the chapter.

Behavior must anchor in a habit to provide sustained benefit:

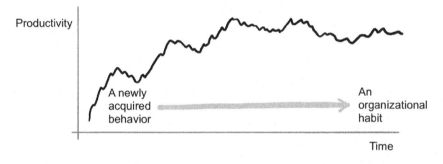

Map 6-28

How is sustainability created?

These actions might help:

- Manage expectations (both of yourself and others). It takes time for a new behavior to form. Months rather than weeks. During this time, solving and removing problems should be the first order of business. There should be no expectation that the intended behavior will actually become a new habit. Most likely it will morph into something quite different from the initial idea. It is very easy to lock yourself into unrealistic outcomes if you don't preserve flexibility in your expectations. Adaptations, and even qualitative shifts, will occur throughout, among enablers and constraints first of all. The trajectory of your complex solution cannot be known upfront, but can only be discovered in the process. You and your stakeholders have to realize that.

- Seek to identify disconnects in the ecosystem early on and repair them. If employees encounter an impediment but the signal never gets to the leadership (who can actually address it) then a newly acquired behavior will die out or degrade into a pathological scenario. The disconnect is not always between employees and their management (although this is where a majority of disconnects appear to be). The disconnect might develop between two dependent teams, a team and their customer, and so on. Chapter 2 is fully dedicated to the subject of identifying disconnects.

- Observe and explore new behaviors and mental models. Earlier in this chapter, we've discussed this topic in more detail.

Ultimately, what counts is not the change that was undertaken but the change that developed into an organizational habit that continually delivers value to the enterprise.

🕮 Taking Action

1 Identify complex bottlenecks hindering your complex tasks/initiatives.

   a Complex bottlenecks usually pertain to human behavior or way of thinking. Look where mindset or behavior hinders achieving beneficial outcomes.

   b Some places to look: actions or ways of thinking of the customer, management, team members, other subject matter experts.

   c Consider interviewing or surveying others in your environment to help identify complex bottlenecks. Here's a simple way to start the inquiry: "In your opinion, what is constraining the performance of our group?" or "What is preventing us from achieving favorable outcomes?" The question does not suggest we are seeking complex bottlenecks, but *any* type of bottleneck. It's just that what constraints sophisticated tasks is often a complex bottleneck. The initial answers that you receive will have to be further explored, of course.

   d Hint: it might look like the missing thing is something simple like tests, or proper defect fixes, or user guidelines. Behind such a superficial constraint there is often a much deeper and more fundamental intangible bottleneck, with a certain behavior or mindset at its core.

2 Once the bottleneck is located, try to identify the ways it manifests (i.e. the paths through which it influences the outcome). Consider exploring this with other participants of the process. Here's a possible initial question to elicit the paths: "How does our bottleneck manifest itself? Exactly how does it impact the outcome?" Think of the answer to this as a bulleted list where each bullet ultimately translates into a path. This is, however, an iterative inquiry that needs to be repeated over and over until you get to some good breakdown of the bottleneck into its paths. Those paths are where the important context resides. This exercise not only helps to better understand the problem but also assists in comprehending a possible solution. (An example of such a breakdown was provided in the first section of this chapter for "Executive team bottlenecked by unproductive, sustained conflict").

3 Describe the idea of the solution.

    a Important: the solution to your bottleneck is a different behavior of the people involved. What would the behavior need to be to eliminate or mitigate the bottleneck? Formulate a hypothesis. Remember that the purpose of this part of the exercise is not to lock yourself down to a specific idea of the target behavior, but instead to accept that the core of a complex solution is the behavior of people rather than things that enable that behavior (such as software, hardware, policy, and so on).

    b Use the breakdown of the bottleneck into paths and sub-paths (see item #2 of this list) to understand the aspects of behavior that are a part of the solution.

    c Observe *current* behavior in detail. Make sure that your assumptions about current behavior are accurate.

4 Explore mental models.

    a What mental models are driving current behavior? How do you know? Research mental models empirically rather than just relying on your speculation. Use approaches described earlier in this chapter.

    b What mental models would be at the foundation of a better behavior? (Remember that the result of this item is only a hypothesis and requires validation).

    c Try to capture both current and possible future mental models in a detailed way. Consider utilizing a "mind map" format (or stick to any other format you find practical).

    d   Make sure that in each case the mental model contains core belief(s). What fundamental motivations do you think those core beliefs are connected with?

5   Tap into the emergence cycle.

    a   Thought experiment: think of the first emergence cycle that would move behavior and mental models closer to the solution. What would that change be in terms of the three components of the cycle?

    b   "Smoke-test" your assumptions: why would a person be compelled to change their mental model (and thus behavior)? Would the behavior align with their underlying motivation?

    c   What enablers and constraints need to be supplied in order to tap into the emergence cycle?

    d   Are there any known barriers to entering the emergence cycle? Is there resistance to change? If so, how would you deal with it?

    e   Welcome surprises! Every time your assumptions about behavior change are incorrect there is a good chance to discover new and possibly beneficial behavior. Stay open-minded so you don't miss an important development.

6   Explore potential solution trajectories.

    a   Try to hypothesize where 3-5 subsequent emergence cycles would get the solution to?

    b   What indicators would you use to determine the direction the solution trajectory is taking?

    c   How would you stay flexible about your solution alternatives?

7   How would you manage expectations about your solution trajectory and the uncertainty associated with it? How long do you think it would take for a new behavior to stabilize and grow into a group habit?

CHAPTER 7

Strategy and Leverage Points

What Is Strategy?

A straightforward task is simple to achieve, and rarely needs any kind of special thinking to accomplish it. A more complex task brings up the question of *how* to do it to achieve a favorable outcome. "Just doing it" is no longer enough, because too many things could go wrong.

In other words, a *strategy* is needed to approach such a task.

We have considered examples of complex tasks in talent management, marketing, sales, business development, software engineering, and other areas of enterprise life. Each requires a strategy to be successful.

Strategy is the way in which system behavior can be vectored toward a favorable outcome.

Strategy may be needed for tasks at any scale. Driving a business to higher revenues and market share requires a business strategy. Creating a new product or enhancing an existing one requires a product strategy. Refactoring an IT asset requires an architecture strategy. Staffing a new initiative requires a hiring strategy. Creating a new search algorithm requires an implementation strategy. Building a strong user community requires a consumer engagement strategy. And so on. It doesn't matter if the task involves thousands of people or a three-person team, they still need a strategy on how to succeed. Size or function of a group is irrelevant in deciding whether a strategy is needed. If a task is complex, it needs a strategy.

That said, strategy is not the exclusive responsibility of executives. Above, we mentioned a small software development team needing an implementation strategy. This is not something executives would provide them with. It is the responsibility of the outcome owner to facilitate the development and execution of the task's strategy. Note that we're not suggesting it's their job to *develop* it but to *facilitate* the process.

What makes a strategy viable?

Here's an old tale that expands on this subject.

The prairie dogs finally had enough of being harassed by various predators and decided to alter their fate. "On the other side of the mountains lives a wise old owl who can give us the right advice," said one of them, and an expedition set off. After walking for three and a half days, they finally made it to the big oak where the owl lived, filling its days with introspection and deep meaning.

"How can we stop predators from harassing us all the time?" asked the bravest prairie dog.

The owl looked at them and then stared off to the horizon, deep in thoughtful consideration. Minutes passed in awkward silence until the owl finally uttered, "You must be like a porcupine. Nobody messes with porcupines!"

The prairie dogs were astounded by the depth of this insight. Going back home they kept talking about it. What an ingenious idea it was, and so simple at the same time. On day two of their journey back home, one of them suddenly stopped and shouted, "Wait! How are we going to be like porcupines?"

The question was so puzzling that they decided to go back to the ancient oak and clarify with the owl how to "be like porcupines".

Once they had returned to the owl's oak, they asked, "Oh, wise owl, we forgot to ask you one little detail: how can we be like porcupines, as you advised?"

The owl frowned. "That's *your* problem. I'm a strategist, not a tactician ..."

As naive as the tale sounds, it has a strong resemblance to a typical strategy process that takes place in many organizations and teams: some version of "becoming porcupines" is baked into a fancy presentation, circulated among stakeholders and communicated to those working on the task execution. The frontline workers wonder how they can "become porcupines", and quickly learn it's *their* problem to figure it out. The workers continue to survive the best they can, while their management thinks the new strategy has geared everyone towards achieving unprecedented outcomes. Most organizations live their own fairytale.

In contrast, here's what Peter did in Example 1, in Chapter 6. He set out to recover trust by demonstrating that he *could* be trusted, by showing he would protect the team when needed, displaying openness, and establishing a good relationship working side by side with the team. Peter only had an idea for the first step rather than a complete plan prepared in advance. Whenever he did, Peter watched carefully for opportunities to demonstrate his trustworthiness to the team. His strategy was implicit and quite intuitive. He did not create a PowerPoint presentation with "quadrants" and "values", and whatnot... Instead, he kept his eyes open to see how the system responded to his action and adapted his strategy whenever an opportunity presented itself. In fact, he managed to *successfully leverage* seemingly adverse factors (when Chris and Natalie were unhappy with his requests to provide the benefit detail for their improvement items).

Turning adversity into an advantage is not a kind of miracle. It's a strategic stance where knowledge revealed by adverse facts is leveraged to drive the system's behavior in a favorable direction.

Underpinning the emergent solution to the problem, Peter's strategy emerged, too. Starting with a very simple strategic decision, he uncovered *leverage points*, one by one, allowing him to build trust with his team, which his predecessors had systematically destroyed.

Viable strategy hinges on the ability to perceive and seize leverage points.

Revealing Existing Leverage Points

Leverage points sit in the center of every strategy, and we will consider a few tools to help in discovering them.

Explore Frontline Context

Leverage points might already exist in the system, and only need to be revealed. A good way to spot leverage is by carefully examining the "frontline" context, by getting input from those who are directly involved or affected by the task. An example in Chapter 2 about the testing strategy problem for a software module rewrite used this strategy. Chapter 3 featured the discovery of important aspects of outcomes directly from the users. Chapter 4 highlighted tools for the discovery of unknowns in the task of skill improvement by surveying employees. Chapter 6 outlined customer surveys to reveal the root of the issue with customer awareness. A lot of valuable information is hidden in the rich frontline context, and this is the first place to look for leverage points.

Assess the Utility of System Behaviors

A lot of things happen within a complex environment. We might be so focused on performing a certain function or executing a particular plan that we fail to notice how different behaviors have a different contribution to the outcome of the system. Even seemingly similar behaviors might manifest a huge difference in the impact on the ultimate results. Triaging a system's behaviors and components based on their utility might reveal impactful leverage points.

Here's an example of this method in use. A product is being marketed to a broad professional audience, but not all the potential buyers are alike. A typical organization licensing a product can make money from the license fee itself, but once the customer has purchased it, there's no direct influence of that customer on the rest of the market. A different type of customer—a consulting organization—works quite differently. A consultant invited to a client organization has credibility just from being invited. If the consultant recommends a product to their clients, it's more likely they will buy it. The direct revenue from consulting organizations (typically small in size) is not much compared to the revenue from "regular" companies, yet their marketing utility is significantly higher. Consulting companies represent a potential leverage point for the producer. To exploit this leverage point, the company might decide to create a marketing campaign targeting consulting firms. They could also use direct sales with consulting organizations, or develop a partnership program for this type of company featuring incentives for referrals.

Use "2+1" Mapping

A simple concept called "2+1" mapping uses a tabular format to represent three important dimensions of the system: two primary ones and one auxiliary one.

A product management team for the enterprise's custom CRM system wants to decide what functionality should be included in the next release of their software. They are pursuing two high-order outcomes: 1) Improve revenue per customer, and 2) Enter new market segments.

They select the two primary dimensions as "New product capabilities" and "User types". The auxiliary dimension is selected as a relative value of each capability to each user type, and the table is filled out by the corresponding scores:

		User types			
		Sales rep	Sales tech support	Sales team leader	Marketing professional
New product capabilities	Issue tracking system	5	8	—	—
	Custom sales materials	8	—	6	6
	Customer experience database	7	7	7	10
	Usage analytics summary	9	10	7	9
	Advanced sales objectives	8	4	8	5
	Demo environment self-service	10	8	—	—

Just filling out this table triggers a lot of critical conversations and important questions about the product, desired outcomes, and constraints, but it also reveals leverage points. In this example, "Usage analytics summary" is a potential leverage point that could be exploited to provide valuable insights to both sales and marketing as to how to better position company's services.

The same product development team might utilize more than one "2+1" perspective, to inform better decisions. A table with the same primary dimensions could be used, but instead of relative values as an auxiliary dimension, each table of the cell could describe exactly *what* should be delivered for that combination of capability and user type. In this case, the auxiliary dimension is the *content* of those capabilities per user type.

It can be helpful to change the primary dimensions, too. The product management team could use "Impediments to sales" and "Key user scenarios" as the new primary dimensions. The auxiliary dimension will be the score indicating how much an impediment affects a scenario.

With the right choice of dimensions, "2+1" can be a very powerful tool because fleshing out various combinations in a single table draws out better thought processes and collaboration.

An *output-outcome matrix* is a special case of the "2+1" diagram, where the primary dimensions of the table are key aspects of output and outcome. It often makes sense to use "value" as the third parameter, in the auxiliary dimension.

An output-outcome matrix for a marketing campaign might be:

		Outcomes		
		Brand awareness	Conversions	Returning customers
	Influencer support	10	7	3
	SEO	5	6	-
	Virtual events	7	5	6
	SMO	7	5	4
Outputs	Automation (sustainment)	-	-	8
	Reviews & Recommendations	4	9	7
	Advanced data analytics	2	8	9

The matrix suggests that involving influencers may offer substantial leverage.

An output-outcome matrix can be effectively coupled with pre-mortem. In this case, pre-mortem can be used to find missing components in the output dimension or help refine value scores. The output-outcome matrix should be filled out first and then enhanced using pre-mortem.

Walk the Outcome Chain

This technique works in both directions – from lower-level to higher-level outcomes and vice versa. Due to common disconnects in outcome chains, owners of outcomes at the lower level of the chain are not exactly familiar with the impact that their immediate outcomes have on the outcomes higher up. And conversely, Outcome Owners that deal with outcomes higher up in the chain, may have limited idea of lower-level outcomes that contribute to the higher-level ones. The goal is to go beyond one's outcomes and learn about the rest of the chain.

Let's take another look at an outcome chain from earlier:

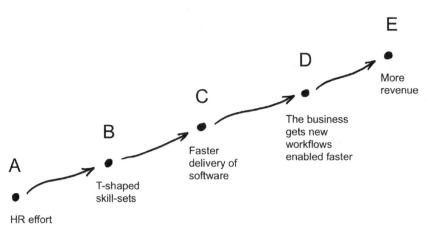

Map 7-1

The company in this example was trying to broaden the skill-sets of employees. We need to determine an effective strategy for achieving this.

It would be helpful for the Outcome Owner of "B" to "walk" up the chain a level or two, and deepen their understanding of the context of "C" and "D". This might reveal leverage points in "B". The Outcome Owner may discover the biggest impediment for an IT professional (node "C") is not the lack of knowledge in how to administer a network switch, but a lack of understanding of the company's vast IT ecosystem and the repercussions of their actions. The leverage then is not in standard training, but in familiarizing IT professionals with the enterprise architecture and establishing direct connections with other teams that support major IT assets in the enterprise.

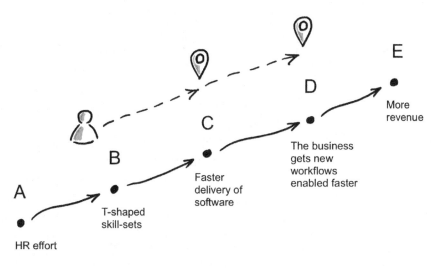

Map 7-2

"Walking the chain" doesn't mean "requesting a formal outcome statement from other outcome owners", but immersing yourself in the context of other outcomes that are connected to yours. We have already used immersion techniques to uncover *immediate* outcomes, but we can use the same technique to go *beyond* the immediate tier.

Analyze Value Paths

We've used value paths to examine the utility or value of a particular asset. Value paths can be extremely useful in identifying leverage points, and so can value moderators.

Here is a detailed value path breakdown with a moderator, detailing the "A-B" link in our outcome chain:

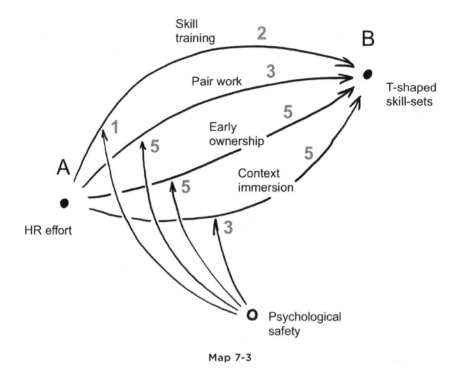

Map 7-3

The map suggests the psychological safety of adopting early ownership and context immersion (with customers and other teams participating in the process) are potential leverage points.

Developing New Leverage Points

Leverage points do not always readily exist, just waiting to be discovered. They could emerge, but the emergence process often has to be actuated and facilitated. We will consider some tools that can help facilitate the emergence of leverage points. All these tools exploit a powerful ability of a complex system for adapting to change in the environment, which can generate novel behaviors that provide leverage. The general approach is:

1   Induce change in the environment

2   See what new behaviors emerge as a result

3   Utilize behaviors that show promise

Let's consider some specific tools that help achieve steps 1-3.

Remove Enabler

Create change by eliminating an existing enabler, or significantly reducing its impact. The system will respond by compensating in some other ways, utilizing other enablers to cover for the deficiency. New system behaviors emerge, and they might represent missing leverage points. Once the new scenarios reveal themselves, the enabler in question can be brought back, but the system will be performing at a new level. A bottlenecked enabler or asset would be a great candidate for this.

Let's consider some examples.

A team wants to improve its poor performance. Most of the team members depend on Lora, an advanced subject matter expert on the team. If they are stuck with their work, Lora can "unstick" them. When they have a question, Lora has an answer. When they need a fresh idea, Lora can probably give them one. Naturally, Lora gets overloaded with requests and people have to wait for those answers, ideas, and thoughts.

Lora is an example of a complex bottleneck. One way to address the bottleneck would be to manage Lora's time more efficiently. Allowing her to focus on the most important thing at any time has the potential to improve team performance to some extent. But other strategies might have a much greater payoff. The "enabler" is Lora, and the help she provides to the team. Instead of trying to streamline dependencies on Lora, we will "remove the enabler" and transfer her to a different, isolated task, separate from her team. The team will have to continue their work without her.

With no easy answers to their questions, the remaining team members are really challenged. They have to discover the answers for themselves. They need to run experiments, rely on trial and error, work as a team to solve problems, master new disciplines, immerse themselves fully in the context of a task at hand. Step by step, their expertise grows in most areas allowing them to succeed with about 80% of tasks without Lora's help. When Lora is brought back to the team, she continues to act in her previous capacity for the remaining 20% of tasks that still depend on her vast prior experience and unique background. The rest of the team has learned to manage most of their tasks on their own and discovered how satisfying it is to be able to complete a sophisticated chunk of work by themselves. This ensures they won't slip back into old behaviors. As a result of the change, the overall team performance improves significantly.

Another example is the marketing team working on a new campaign. Instead of following their usual pathway of creating some content that includes both graphics and text copy, the team creates two independent versions of the campaign. In one they only use images, and in the other they only use text. Without text, images must convey the right message in a completely different way. Without graphics, words must hold a lot more expressive power. Because of the constraint, new techniques begin to arise on both sides. If the constraint is then dropped, and powerfully expressive images and text could be used together, the effectiveness of the campaign may be elevated to a whole new level.

Amplify Constraining Factor

When there is a factor that imposes a constraint on the system, amplify it. The system should respond with novel behaviors that might offer a qualitative shift towards the desired outcome. Use caution to avoid amplifying an adverse factor in a way that jeop-ardizes the outcome. A trade-off of some sort is usually required.

The following example can demonstrate the technique in action.

Marketing campaigns need to be adjusted to accommodate a specific customer group, partnership, or industry event, leading to multiple change requests. The team responsible for these changes struggles with modifying existing campaign materials. The team usually holds off these requests until a critical number of them stacks up, and then does all the changes across all required assets in a single sweep. This approach slows down the organization but also produces numerous quality issues. Everyone just wants to get this task over with as fast as possible, leaving no room for proper quality control. The team even asked their boss to minimize the number of change requests. The higher level of the organization has decided to apply strict prioritization to change requests, and not even consider those that don't match the "importance criteria". Their team leader had to adopt a new responsibility of rejecting as many requests for change as possible.

The change requests are an obvious constraining factor. Amplifying the constraint means accepting a more frequent rate of change. An interesting transformation happens as the team accepts the challenge and change requests are no longer put on hold. At first, the team is overwhelmed. But some team members notice it is so hard to update existing media project files because of the naviga-tion problem inside those files. Graphical objects are multi-layered constructs and each layer holds a fraction of the whole graphic. Habitually, layers were created without proper labeling, making it very difficult to navigate through the components of a graphical object. At the moment of creation, the designer keeps everything in their head, but after a while, nobody remembers what elements were grouped together into layers or why. An idea came up to start properly labeling the layers. But it was quickly discovered that assigning meaningful names is far not always possible because the way the elements have been grouped together did not always convey much meaning and rather was a matter of convenience at the moment of creation. After a while of trial and error, the group learned that they are much better off if they create a layer only when it corresponds to a meaningful property of the final graphical asset – something that can be clearly articulated. And if it can be articulated, it can be properly labeled, too. Then they have decided to go over all media files they could think of and update them correspondingly. But that turned out to be an enormous effort. So, a better solution emerged: the team would only make a sweep for the 10% of the most frequently updated files. The rest would be updated only when a change request came in for that particular file. As a result of applying these new practices for a while, the team developed an ability to complete change requests 3-5 times faster. With improving the process the team also became much more comfortable dealing with change. These requests were no longer so daunting, and became a reasonable professional challenge, with success giving a sense of accomplishment. That in itself put an end to quality problems as the team no longer just sought to "get it done with", but aspired to create a quality result that would make an impact.

Developing a new leverage point has one fundamental advantage over uncovering an existing one: instead of trying to eliminate or mitigate a bottleneck, we circumvent it. A dramatically new system behavior resulting from such leverage may get the system's performance to a whole new level. Its innovative nature has the potential for producing a dramatic qualitative shift.

Explore and Exploit Adversity

Every problem encountered in the context of a complex task reveals a discrepancy between existing mental models of reality and the reality itself. It exposes what has been missed, and that is often a leverage point. So, instead of getting frustrated with problems that pop up during a complex task, we want to use the opportunity to reveal unknown leverage.

Here are some examples.

The first example is the T-shaping of employees where, as a part of the strategy, the company has decided to invest in skill training. The data from individual teams revealed that almost nobody is operating in any new capacity, and people are staying within the boundaries of their previous skill-sets. The problem turns out to be due to a lack of psychological safety: working in a new capacity is fraught with visible errors that will have an impact at the next performance review. The missing psychological safety is where the leverage point lies and it is quite easy to discover if the failure with T-shaping is regarded as an improvement opportunity rather than just a mishap.

The next example is in the field of marketing where a company is trying to promote a new service to existing customers. Their advertising campaign doesn't make much impact. Upon further investigation it turned out that the way the new service is articulated created ambiguity, making some customers think it was just a refreshed advertisement of the existing services. Some of the surveyed customers also indicated they weren't actually using other companies' services but this new service makes a lot of sense to them. The wording behind the campaign is changed. The new service will now be marketed to the general public as well as existing customers.

Finding a leverage point is not the same as solving it. The problem may bring awareness to an entirely new opportunity, but only by trying to solve the problem in the first place.

Strategy Diffusion and Culture

Culture embodies extremely powerful forces governing almost every aspect of the group's life, whether it is a large organization or a small team. Cultural scenarios emerge firmly tied into individual and group motivation, pertinent to an environment. Most of these scenarios remain hidden, silently moving system behavior in a certain direction. Introducing a change without understanding the nuanced culture of a particular organization or team is almost certain to backfire.

This often happens with an "imposed" strategy. No matter how "good" the desired strategy might sound, if it's not internalized at the cultural level, the existing culture will override it:

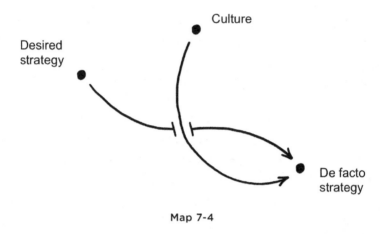

Map 7-4

A strategy is potent only when it is embraced in culture.

As an example, if an organization's hiring strategy becomes "hire the best of the best on the market", and the organization has a strong culture of centralized control overspending, the strategy will likely fail. Similarly, a team with a culture of narrow specialization will struggle to embrace the strategy of T-shaping to boost performance. Likewise, a department with a culture of pursuing "predictability" will have serious trouble realizing the strategy of innovation.

But this is not to say that poor cultural scenarios should squash good ideas. Sometimes an organizational shift has to be made. And if the shift has to be "imposed" from the top, it is not going to be achieved as a result of wishful thinking, a memo, or a pretty PowerPoint presentation, outlining the wonders of the new direction. The intended strategy is only the *input*. It still has to go through the natural process of internalization, which requires facilitation, and what ultimately comes out of the initial strategic intent may be quite different from the original intent.

There is no accident, that strategy gets inevitably ingrained in the culture and that it is *the only actual strategy* that influences the outcome. Reliance on culture as a powerful mechanism to embrace strategy lies at the foundation of our evolutionary success as species. The simpler the species, the more it relies on innate behavior, and the less capacity it has to learning new behaviors. More advanced species, on the opposite, have high behavioral plasticity and the ability to learn from experience. Moreover, some developed an ability to social learning or learning from experiences of others in the population. This trait is particularly well-developed developed in humans, and has a tremendous impact in terms of survival. If behaviors are no longer hardwired, they can alter without necessarily changing the "hardware" that "runs" them. This creates a powerful basis for adaptation that is orders of magnitude faster than biological evolution. As a result, most of the behaviors are running on "software". That "software"—a product of collective trial and error internalized by each individual—is what we call *culture*. And while a lot of survival strategies are encoded in "hardware" for simpler animals, for humans strategies predominantly develop in "software", i.e. the cultural layer.

The de facto strategy emerges regardless of whether it originated from an imposed strategic intent or developed from the inside out. The primary strategic intent can sometimes be imposed, but it has to go through the same emergence spiral we discussed earlier in Chapter 6. The result will be an internalization of the initial message, which will be adapted and adjusted thousands of times. The initial strategy will not adapt to existing mental models, and neither will mental models adapt to meet the declared strategy. Instead, the initial message *and* mental models are going to coevolve to form an updated culture that encapsulates the new strategy.

To facilitate a productive process of such strategy diffusion, it is important to be able to see if the strategy:

1   Is actually being internalized

2   Helps move toward a favorable outcome.

Both items 1 and 2 must be measured early in the process and those measurements need to be protected from the influence of bias because those who introduce the new strategy in a typical enterprise environment are also the ones who evaluate the performance of the people applying the strategy.

Static vs. Dynamic Leverage

Some leverage points may be long-lived, but leverage often emerges dynamically, diminishing quickly, and it is important to act while the window of opportunity is open. This dictates an important aspect of effectively operating in a complex environment: take advantage of the leverage point and move to the next one.

The organization must accept the dynamic nature of its strategy and routinely explore and assess new leverage points. Leverage expires over time, and if the organization does not pay attention, the strategy becomes outdated and outcomes can no longer be productively achieved.

Here's an example of a natural progression from one leverage point to another:

A company decides to enhance the employee benefit program so it can attract the best talent on the market. In time, other companies on the market start to catch up and the new benefit program no longer differentiates the company from other players. A new leverage point is needed. The company updates its expertise levels and career growth process to allow for more flexibility and recognition of achievement. The newly created slots get saturated in time, and the opportunity to improve fades. These leverage points continue to benefit the existing employees, but no longer entice new employees to join the company. This creates the need for the next leverage point. And the process continues on...

Leverage points are dynamic but they don't change on a daily basis. It could take months or even quarters before the impact of a leverage point significantly diminishes. But it is going to happen sooner or later and sustaining the runway of future leverage points, constantly scouting out better opportunities, is a crucial element of leading the organization into a better future.

Taking Action

1   For the initiatives you are involved in, what leverage points can you name? (Is there empirical evidence these are really leverage points? If you can't name them it just means you must discover them.)

2   Use methods described in this chapter to discover leverage points. (Consider exploring the frontline context, assessing the utility of system behaviors, using "2+1" mapping, walking the outcome chain, and analyzing value paths.)

3   For the existing leverage points, how could you exploit them effectively? Are they already being exploited?

4   Develop new leverage points. (Consider removing an existing enabler, amplifying a constraining factor, exploring and exploiting adversity.)

5   What cultural scenarios prevent you from exploiting certain leverage points? What corrective action would you take? (Note that the point here is neither to adjust culture to leverage points nor leverage points to culture, but rather to facilitate the emergence of updated scenarios and leverage points that would provide beneficial outcomes.)

References and Commentary

Interaction Maps

Interaction maps are anchored in graph theory. A graph is a powerful way to focus on connections in a system, rather than the elements themselves. Graph theory is commonly used in economics, sociology, computer science, biology, and many other domains. [1] represents a brief overview of the theory.

Interaction maps were also influenced by:

- Causal loop diagrams, which is a key tool in systems dynamics [2].
- Impact maps described in [3] by Gojko Adzic who seems to have borrowed the concept from effect maps introduced by Balic and Ottersten in [4].
- Intermediate objectives maps and reality trees explored by H. William Dettmer in [5].

Disconnects and Bottlenecks, Their Discovery

A good foundation for understanding bottlenecks is the *Theory of Constraints* (TOC) by Eliyahu Goldratt [6, 7].

A conceptually similar perspective on bottlenecks is used in Lean which takes its roots in Toyota Production System (TPS) [8, 9]. However, it has to be noted that despite conceptual alignment, Lean has a number of distinctions with TOC.

Taiichi Ohno, one of the founding fathers of the TPS, paid a lot of attention to discovery through thorough observation [10], the foundational practice for the notion of Gemba [11, 12].

The value-action gap, mentioned in both Chapters 2 and 6, refers to the inconsistency between intention and actual behavior [13, 14].

A good study on the power of open-ended queries, conducted by John Geer [15], shows how effectively open-ended questions reveal important insights from respondents.

Outcomes

Josh Seiden's book [16] is a good, quick read on the importance of focusing on outcomes.

The "impacts" [3] and "effects" [4] mentioned above represent a concept similar to outcomes. Also, desired and undesired effects are used alongside outcomes in [5] as a part of current and future reality trees.

User stories [17], in their original form, can be viewed as a way to connect outputs to outcomes. It can be argued that a properly written user story connects outputs to both immediate and second-order outcomes. Its classic format is: "As a <user>, I can <action>, so that <benefit>". The second clause is often the user behavior that the system is supposed to enable (the immediate outcome), and the third clause describes the benefit that the behavior brings about (the next-order outcome). Additionally, the first-person voice in which user stories are written fosters empathy. It must be noted, however, that this only works when a user story *directly* describes the consumer context. In large organizations, user stories can end up being used as "the lowest-level work items" and end up being disconnected from the actual user context.

Design thinking [18] is an example of a domain with well-developed use of consumer empathy to drive better solutions.

Probing

In Chapter 4 we mentioned that perception is conditioned by intention (which might be explicit or implicit). Physiological needs have been proven to bias perception [19]. Monetary incentives likewise appear to condition perception [20]. An experiment conducted on "inattentional blindness" involved researchers asking observers to keep count of passes made by a group of people passing around a basketball [21]. A person wearing a gorilla suit crosses the room at a certain point, and almost half the participants fail to notice the gorilla. This is a great demonstration of how focusing on one particular thing alters perception and inhibits the ability to perceive signals that do not align with the goal.

Confirmation bias is one of the cognitive biases mentioned in Chapter 4 as a serious concern when dealing with complex tasks. Cognitive biases are described in depth in Daniel Kahneman's book [22]. The book expands on the subject of jumping to conclusions, described in Chapter 4. Kahneman describes the role of cognitive strain and cognitive ease in decision making and seeking coherent stories. The two systems introduced in the book—System 1 and System 2—are worthwhile mentioning and represent a very convenient conceptual model to think about cognitive processes in humans.

The Cynefin framework [23], created by Dave Snowden, provides a way to reason about the complexity of the ecosystem one operates in. The framework emphasizes the importance of probing when operating in a complex domain, recommending "probe-sense-respond" as modus operandi in this case. It stresses the importance of emergence as a way complex adaptive systems evolve. The HBR article [24] provides some examples of applying Cynefin framework to decision-making.

A powerful way of probing in software development was included as a part of Extreme Programming methodology in the form of Spikes (sometimes referred to as Solution Spikes) [25].

More generically, Agile software development heavily relies on probing by building increments of the solution [26]. There is undoubtedly a great advantage in having probing instilled as a part of the way of operating. At the same time, it is important to note that Agile focuses primarily on validating the producer's ability to build software that meets customer need. Validation of business outcomes receives a lot less attention in Agile and commonly requires borrowing tools from other disciplines (such as Lean Startup).

Lean Startup [27] relies heavily on probing for business outcomes. The methodology also highlights the important mechanism of Leading Indicators as a part of "Innovation Accounting", a way to reason about future value.

The concept of known vs. unknown unknowns belongs to Donald H. Rumsfeld [28], but receives great attention as a part of the Cynefin framework, mentioned earlier.

Pre-mortem [29, 22], or proactive hindsight, was proven effective by a group of researchers: Deborah J. Mitchell, Jay Russo, and Nancy Pennington. The method, however, was first presented by Gary A. Klein [30].

An interesting article [31] demonstrates the negative economic impact of late defect detection in software development.

A useful perspective on operating in an environment of uncertainty is offered by Donald Reinertsen [32]. One of the key principles he proposes for the task of product development is "Understand and exploit uncertainty".

More detail on the concept of the Red Team can be found in [33].

In Chapters 3 and 4, it has been mentioned that the structure of organizations and teams is intimately connected with their ability to focus on outcomes and effectively probe for unknowns. In particular, the fragmented structure of teams within the organization was named as one of the impediments to outcome focus and organizational learning. To learn more about various approaches to structuring organizations and teams, the following sources can be useful. Scaled Agile Framework® (SAFe®) thoroughly utilizes the concept of value streams—as well as the number of other subservient constructs—to organize knowledge workers around value [34]. Large-Scale Scrum (also referred to as LeSS [35]) emphasizes the importance of structuring teams around requirements areas [36]. Additionally, in their book "Team Topologies" [37], Matthew Skelton and Manuel Pais explore a broad variety of aspects that influence productive team structures.

Relative Business Value

In his book, "The Art of Business Value", Mark Schwartz [38] explores in depth the complexity of the value discovery process. He provides numerous examples, showing that value definition cannot be achieved within a simplistic, univariate framework. He also points out the crucial connections of value to the structure and culture of organizations.

In "Agile Software Requirements" [39], Dean Leffingwell points out the complexity of value definition for software features and the inherent difficulty and danger in assigning financial value. This sentiment is emphasized by Mark Schwartz. The approach lies in using relative numbers instead of the financial expression of value. Using relative numbers allows crucial aspects of business value to be revealed that would otherwise remain undiscovered.

The concept of relative scoring of value ultimately found numerous applications as a part of the Scaled Agile Framework® [34].

Value Paths

The notion of value paths, as a foundation for value discovery, is rooted in a number of mathematical concepts. Before we go into a deeper level of detail, it is important to note that in its simplest form using value paths is based on the idea of a multi-dimensional vector (rather than a number) in assessing the value of an asset. Complex assets are very multifaceted and thus the apparatus that would allow to effectively deal with them would have to be, by design, multifaceted, too.

The following are the areas that influenced the approach behind value paths:

Optimization Theory

The idea of optimizing system performance to achieve higher benefit isn't new. At the intuitive level, it's probably as old as humankind itself. But as a separate, formal discipline, it appeared in the form of what we know today as the theory of optimization. Quite a breakthrough in this domain happened early in the XX century with the development of a specific domain called *linear programming* [40] and built on big names such as John von Neumann, Leonid Kantorovich, T. C. Koopmans, and George B. Dantzig. Kantorovich and Koopmans ultimately received a Nobel Prize for their contribution to the theory of the optimum allocation of economic resources [41]. And that shouldn't be surprising. The fast economic growth driven by the scientific and technological progress in the XX century posed a number of resource planning challenges. The two World Wars and the subsequent Cold War imposed additional challenges related to military operations, technology race, and grand strategies.

In its simplest notation, a classical problem of linear programming could be expressed as follows:

Maximize function:

$$f = c_1 \cdot x_1 + c_2 \cdot x_2 + \ldots + c_N \cdot x_N,$$

given the constraints:

$$a_{11} \cdot x_1 + a_{12} \cdot x_2 + \ldots + a_{1N} \cdot x_N \leq b_1$$
$$a_{21} \cdot x_1 + a_{22} \cdot x_2 + \ldots + a_{2N} \cdot x_N \leq b_2$$
$$\ldots$$
$$a_{M1} \cdot x_1 + a_{M2} \cdot x_2 + \ldots + a_{MN} \cdot x_N \leq b_M,$$

with all variables x_1, x_2, ..., x_N being positive.

Many economic problems could be approximated this way, including problems in resource planning, routing, investment management, and so on.

It is quite easy to spot that the expression we used for the aggregate value of an asset looks exactly like f where c_1, c_2, ..., c_N are the importance scores and x_1, x_2, ..., x_N are the capacity scores for the value paths. We stated the problem in a more simplistic manner, however. Instead of dealing with a pretty complex set of N-dimensional points $(x_1, x_2, ..., x_N)$ that satisfy all the inequalities above, we assumed that we simply have to make an optimal choice over a finite set of options that correspond to a number of asset configurations (picking the best job candidate out of a few possible ones or selecting an optimal software package from among a few vendors, and so on). In the general case, the linear programming problem involves quite a sophisticated solution that may be achieved using a so-called simplex method; something we have avoided due to the above-mentioned simplifications. Function f has multiple names that established over time. It's usually referred to as a goal function, objective function, or utility function. Multidimensional points of the form $(x_1, x_2, ..., x_N)$ constitute a so-called vector space or linear space [42], again depending on a naming convention. Vector spaces are fundamental to a large number of scientific disciplines and we will come back to them a few more times in the remaining portion of this book. Linear algebra is one of the primary disciplines that studies basic proprieties of vector spaces.

A great two-dimensional visualization for linear optimization can be found in [43].

Nonlinear optimization [44] often represents a much broader set of models that may be a better fit for the problem at hand. We used nonlinear utility functions in Chapter 5 when talking about progressive and regressive yield. There we took advantage of power function as a basis for modeling out some nonlinear behavior.

An important caution: *applying any model requires relentless probing and empirical validation.* And optimization theory, whether linear or nonlinear, is no exception to this rule. It is very easy to get excited about a tool that appears to fit the multi-dimensional nature of the problem, and yet fail to notice that the dimensions and the scores are defined in a completely speculative manner.

Riesz Spaces

In simple terms, a Riesz space (named after Hungarian mathematician Frigyes Riesz) is a vector space with an order defined on it [45]. (The order must "align" with the linear property of the space.) Having an "order" means that we can compare certain vectors to one another. The importance of this concept is fundamental, as enterprise economics hinges on the ability to assess and compare alternatives (for investments, solutions, patterns, strategies, and so on). The theory of Riesz spaces is one of the strong reasons why linear forms were used to approximate the value of a complex asset. More specifically, it is due to the Birkhoff theorem [46]. In layman's terms, this theorem suggests that every order in a finite-dimensional Riesz space has a "sibling" order that can be broken down into lexicographical components [47], i.e. components that work the same way as we order words in a dictionary, only with numbers instead of letters and vectors instead of words. (Due to excessive complexity, we are not citing the full version of the theorem here.) We will just note, that due to the theorem, every order can be substituted by one or more linear forms, similar to a utility function considered in the previous subsection.

Infinite-Dimensional Spaces

While in all examples in Chapter 5 we only dealt with finite-dimensional vectors, it has been noted that fractal value paths are composed of a virtually endless sequence of subpaths at an ever deeper level. In other words, we always dealt with a finite approximation of virtually infinite-dimensional vectors. And while we haven't used the infinite number of components at all, we took advantage of this "infinite depth" indirectly when applying the Pareto Unpacking method to value paths. "Unpacking" was simply a transition from a less accurate to a more accurate model by bringing in additional dimensions of the problem where it mattered most. Although we only used infinite-dimensional spaces in an implicit way, they form a substantial body of knowledge serving various domains. While finite-dimensional spaces can be thought of as sets of vectors, the elements of infinite-dimensional spaces can rather be thought of as functions from one infinite set into another [48].

A specific example of an infinite-dimensional space that most people have likely dealt with in school (but probably had no idea that it was an infinite-dimensional vector space) is the space of polynomials [49], i.e. expressions like $3 + 2x + x^4$ or $2 - x + 3.5x^6 + 2x^7$ and so on. The elements $1, x, x^2, ..., x^N, ...$ form an infinite "basis" for this space.

Infinite-dimensional spaces have another important characteristic. Complex behaviors are much better described qualitatively than quantitatively. But a qualitative description (a story, a chunk of text, or narrative) conveys a large number of subtextual parameters. And as a captured story gets extended and further refined, it encompasses more and more variables. Even though every specific representation of the story is finite, there is virtually no limit to depth and refinement that can be incrementally achieved.

Dot Product

The mechanism used throughout Chapter 5 for assessing value is the dot product, sometimes also referred to as the scalar product, of two vectors that have an equal number of dimensions [50]. A dot product a·b of two vectors $a = (a_1, ..., a_N)$ and $b = (b_1, ..., b_N)$ is defined as follows:

$a·b = a_1·b_1 + ... + a_N· b_N.$

The linear goal function, referenced earlier in this section, is an example of the dot product. Respectively, all linear expressions for the total value of an asset used in Chapter 5, are a dot product of importance and capability vectors for that asset.

The dot product is so important to assessing value in complex, multivariate cases because it is sensitive to how well aligned the two vectors are. When there's a mismatch between the importance scores and the capability scores (in other words, the asset is not what's needed for the outcome, see Map 5-16), the value of the dot product will be quite low. In particular, the dot product of orthogonal vectors equals zero. And on the opposite, when the two vectors are well-aligned, the value of the dot product is higher, getting the highest possible value when the "structure" of the two vectors ideally matches.

The dot product was also used in Pareto Unpacking. Essentially, as a part of the method, an *algebraic* product of a path's importance and capability scores was extended to a *dot* product over its subpaths, as a way of achieving higher granularity.

Power Law

A power law [51] is a relationship between two quantities x and y of the form: $y = ax^b$, where a and b are real constants. Many statistical relationships follow a power law with parameter $b < -1$. The well known Pareto Principle (also referred to as the 80/20-rule, [52]) is an example of a probability distribution function that is based on a power law. (Note that we say that probability distributions are "based" on, but not exactly equal to, power law. A probability density function that is based on power law has to have a "prefix" supplied by some other function for lower values of the random variable. This is because otherwise, it would not be a legitimate probability density function, given that ax^b exceeds 1 for lower values of x when $b < -1$.)

In Chapter 5, we assumed that we can apply the Pareto Principle to value paths and their subpaths, to be able to use Pareto

Unpacking. While there is no scientific proof that the Pareto Principle could be universally applied to any area of human activity, there exists some evidence in support of the assumption that knowledge structures and skill-set structures may follow a power law distribution. Louridas, Spinellis, and Vlachos, researchers of the University of Athens, show that connectivity in software components follows a power law [53]. Importantly enough, this relationship does not depend on the scale and applies to both micro and macro levels. The implication of this is that the importance of knowledge of different library functions and constructs follows a similar distribution. That's exactly what's needed to be able to apply Pareto Unpacking.

Such research is available in case of software knowledge/skill areas because it is one of the few domains where a certain type of connections can be easily captured and analyzed. (Software source code can be programmatically scanned for dependencies.) But software development is far from the only example. Knowledge structures seem to follow power laws in many other instances. For example, WordNet, a lexical network of English words, also follows a power law distribution in terms of connections [54]. The use of professional concepts also appears to follow power law distribution [55][56]. Additionally, as per a little research of my own, topics within various Stack Exchange [57] domains appear to follow power law distribution in terms of frequency. (The randomly selected domains were: GIS, Graphic Design, Writing, Video Production, Law, Sound Design, Project Management, SharePoint, Salesforce, Unix and Linux, and the top 36 topics in each were selected for frequency analysis.)

Emergent Solutions

A great example of emergent solutions is the evolution of biological species [58]. Driven by selective pressures (such as natural and sexual selection), it provides multiple examples of both qualitative shifts and subsequent adaptations, mentioned in Chapter 6. (An important parallel exists between these concepts and their evolutionary counterparts: disruptive [59] and stabilizing [60] selection, respectively.) Maintaining multiple solution options is inherently paralleled with how inheritance and variation shape the continual development of a species. There are other interesting parallels that go beyond what has been considered in this book. For example, horizontal gene transfer [61] provides a great example of how various aspects may be interchanged across solution options. Evolution also serves as a great example of the dialectic interaction of diversity, as an intrinsic trait of complex systems, *and* commonality that emerges under the pressure of dominant environmental forces or constraints. The abundant evidence of the former manifests in a vast variety of species on the extremely broad phylogenetic tree [62]. The evidence for the latter is in convergent evolution [63], a good example of which could be parallel evolution of vision in species whose common ancestors did not have this sense organ. Additionally, the evolution of species teaches us another great lesson: complex systems develop in layers where new capabilities grow on top of something that is empirically proven (as opposed to being frivolously redesigned from the ground up every time a new idea pops up).

While there are huge similarities, there are also distinctions between the evolution of species and the emergence of complex solutions in the enterprise context. The most profound one is in that the driver for evolution—mutation—is a result of random forces, while solutions in the enterprise context can be advanced in a more purposeful manner. This fact contains a powerful opportunity but also a dangerous pitfall. The opportunity is that the process of emergence can be effectively vectored towards a highly productive outcome because the collective intelligence of those driving the emergence of the solution might find many useful shortcuts. The pitfall is that this may easily turn into a mechanistic approach to dealing with a complex system, where everything gets designed to a specification and there's no viable selective pressure for ideas, as empirical evidence gets conveniently replaced by cognitive bias.

Emergence loop, mentioned in Chapter 6, has multiple concepts at its foundation:

- The Knowledge Spiral introduced by Nonaka and Takeuchi [64]. The cycle that underlies the model is also known as the SECI model [65].
- PDCA cycle [66]
- OODA loop [67]

It has been mentioned that mental models are not stored in one place but rather spread across multiple circuits in the brain. A good place to learn more about the subject (including the empirical evidence of the mentioned fact) is the following paper: [68].

Enablers and constraints, utilized when talking about both probing and facilitating solution emergence, are used in the most generic sense of the term. The notion, however, was influenced by a number of concepts. Dettmer [5] uses critical success factors and necessary conditions as contributing components in intermediate objectives maps. The notion of enablers is extensively used in the Scaled Agile Framework®[34], however, in more specific context as factors that influence the ability to build software, hardware, and other systems (in this case, enablers typically are architectural or infrastructure work, research, and experimentation). Snowden [69] emphasizes the notion of constraints and utilizes interventions as a way to influence the dynamics of a complex adaptive system, as a part of Cynefin framework.

The concept of delaying non-urgent decisions takes its root from the idea of delaying commitment, described by Mary Poppendieck [70].

Vertical slicing, mentioned in Chapter 6, has its origins in Agile methods, more specifically Extreme Programming [71], [72]. Also, the concept of Minimum Viable Product (MVP), popularized by Eric Ries [27], extends the notion to a tool for testing business hypotheses. Note, however, that in Chapter 6 there's a strong emphasis on vertical slicing as a way to advance the *entire* ecosystem as opposed to any isolated component (like a software system that is being developed)

Multiple solution options come from Lean Product Development [9] as a method to facilitate fast experimentation.

The concept of (solution) trajectory is borrowed from the Dynamical Systems Theory [73]. The overall concept of the state space (where the trajectory unfolds) is quite useful, as well as some other concepts. However, serious caution must be taken: in complex environments, the underlying ruleset is not known and thus the trajectory cannot be determined in an upfront manner (unlike a common implicit assumption in Dynamical Systems Theory).

In Chapter 6 it has been mentioned that sometimes a wrong mental model provides a better path to favorable outcomes. As surprising as it sounds, it has been proven by a large number of empirical examples. A very typical example is connected to a natural propensity to underestimate the complexity and amount of work involved in a task. As a result, some great endeavors are driven to completion that otherwise would have not even gotten started. In his talk [74], Daniel Kahneman mentions an account of an influential decision-maker: "If we knew exactly how much things would cost, we'd never do anything".

Strategy

In Chapter 7 we mentioned that the proportion of learned vs. innate behavior in animals increases from simpler to more complex species. Indeed, simple organisms like bacteria [75] have no nervous system and can't learn new behaviors. (They, however, do acquire new innate behaviors over a number of generations [76].) Yet some of the simplest organisms that feed on bacteria and have a nervous system, such as the roundworm, already demonstrate an ability to learn [77]. (For example, they learn to avoid pathogenic bacteria they were previously exposed to.) Cultural learning is a trait characteristic to more complex species but does not only take place in humans, as it has been believed for quite a long time. Cultural learning, even though in simpler forms, is present in primates, whales, and even birds [78].

The "Remove Enabler" method for developing new capabilities has multiple examples in different domains. So, sensory compensation [79], for instance, facilitates the development of the other available senses if one of the senses stops working. The evolution of biological species also provides ample examples of "shifting priorities" across different capabilities depending on the long-term change in the environment. "Remove enabler" is also tightly connected with the notion of exaptation [80]. Exaptation is a process of emergence of a qualitatively new utility to an existing trait.

An interesting example of a negative system dynamic that can be approached with the "Remove Enabler" method is the Resource Curse [81]. It takes place when an entity (a country, for example) possessing an abundant resource tends to struggle economically.

The "2+1" method of discovering leverage points can be viewed as an advanced form of incidence matrix [82] of a graph. That being said, every interaction map has its incidence matrix, and in some cases switching between the two views can offer productive insights. Additionally, Specification by Example, popularized by Gojko Adzic as a method for refining one's understanding of product requirements, and often used in test-case development [83], teaches us about the usefulness of a detailed conversation mediated by the tabular, highly visible format of information.

The "Amplify Constraining Factor" method is conceptually related to "Remove Enabler" in the sense that they both place additional load on the system thus fostering adaptation. The difference is in how that extra load is being achieved. A sentiment similar to "Amplify Constraining Factor" appears in [84] and is stated as "If it hurts, do it more frequently, and bring the pain forward", and is a foundational idea to process improvement in areas such as Continuous Delivery, and, more generically, DevOps [85].

A great example of the "Amplify Constraining Factor" is a constraint-led approach broadly utilized in sports training [86]. Training at altitude is another common example in sports [87].

"Explore and Exploit Adversity" is significantly moderated by the psychological safety of the environment. Overall, psychological safety has been mentioned multiple times in the book as one of the critical factors in achieving various enterprise outcomes. A good place to learn more would be [88] and [89]. Like most complex assets, psychological safety influences outcomes in a highly context-dependent way and requires other balancing factors. So, for example, if psychological safety is not coupled with a strong motivation, unfavorable outcomes might be produced.

An interesting perspective on leverage points can be found in [90]. Twelve leverage points are considered as the places where system intervention can be facilitated. While representing a useful set of considerations, it is important to note that in inherently complex systems, leverage points may appear *anywhere* and in potentially any form and shape, and are not constrained to a pre-defined set of possibilities. Contextual discovery of leverage points is always required.

Reference List

[1]   Graph Theory. Wikipedia. https://en.wikipedia.org/wiki/
      Graph_theory.

[2]   Causal Loop Diagram. Wikipedia. https://en.wikipedia.org/wiki/
      Causal_loop_diagram.

[3]   Adzic, G. (2012). Impact Mapping. Provoking Thoughts.

[4]   Balic, M. & Ottersen, I. (2007). Effect Managing IT. Copenhagen
      Business School Pr.

[5]   Dettmer, W. (2007). The Logical Thinking Process: A Systems
      Approach to Complex Problem Solving.

[6]   Goldratt, E. (2004). The Goal: A Process of Ongoing Improvement.
      North River Press; 3rd Revised Edition.

[7]   Goldratt, E. (2002). Critical Chain. North River Press.

[8]   Womack, J. P. & Jones, D. T. (2003). Lean Thinking: Banish Waste and
      Create Wealth in Your Corporation, Revised and Updated. Free Press.

[9]   Ward, A. C. & Sobek D. K. (2014). Lean Product and Process
      Development. Lean Enterprise Institute, Inc. 2nd Edition.

[10] Nakane, J. & Hall, R. W. Ohno's Method: Creating a Survival Work
      Culture. https://www.ame.org/sites/default/files/target_arti-
      cles/02-18-1-Ohnos_Method.pdf.

[11] Gemba. Wikipedia. https://en.wikipedia.org/wiki/Gemba.

[12] Toyota's Top Engineer on How to Develop Thinking People.
      Gemba Academy. https://blog.gembaacademy.com/2008/08/04/
      toyotas_top_engineer_on_how_to_develop_thinking_pe/.

[13] Value-action Gap. Wikipedia. https://en.wikipedia.org/wiki/
      Value-action_gap.

[14] Attitude-behavior Consistency. Wikipedia. https://en.wikipedia.org/
      wiki/Attitude-behavior_consistency.

[15] Geer, J. G. (1991). Do open-ended questions measure "salient"
      issues? Public Opinion Quarterly, 55(3), 360–370.

[16]   Seiden, J. (2019). Outcomes Over Output: Why Customer Behavior Is the Key Metric for Business.

[17]   User Story. Wikipedia. https://en.wikipedia.org/wiki/User_story.

[18]   Design Thinking. Wikipedia. https://en.wikipedia.org/wiki/Design_thinking.

[19]   Radel, R. & Clement-Guillotin, C. (2012). Evidence of Motivational Influences in Early Visual Perception: Hunger Modulates Conscious Access. Psychological Science. 23, 232.

[20]   Wilbertz, G. Van Slooten, J., & Sterzer, P. (2014). Reinforcement of Perceptual Inference: Reward and Punishment Alter Conscious Visual Perception During Binocular Rivalry. Frontiers in Psychology.

[21]   Simons, D. J. & Chabris, C. F. (1999). "Gorillas in Our Midst: Sustained Inattentional Blindness for Dynamic Events". Perception. 28 (9): 1059-1074.

[22]   Kahneman, D. (2013). Thinking Fast and Slow. Farrar, Straus and Giroux.

[23]   Cynefin Framework. Wikipedia. https://en.wikipedia.org/wiki/Cynefin_framework.

[24]   Snowden D. J. & Boone, M. E. (2007). A Leader's Framework for Decision Making. Harvard Business Review; Nov 2007 Issue, 68. (Available at: https://hbr.org/2007/11/a-leaders-framework-for-decision-making)

[25]   Cunningham, W. Create a Spike Solution. http://www.extremeprogramming.org/rules/spike.html.

[26]   Manifesto for Agile Software Development. https://agilemanifesto.org.

[27]   Ries, E. (2011). The Lean Startup: How Today's Entrepreneurs Use Continuous Innovation to Create Radically Successful Businesses. Currency.

[28]   DoD News Briefing - Secretary Rumsfeld and Gen. Myers. U. S. Department of Defense. https://archive.defense.gov/Transcripts/Transcript.aspx?TranscriptID=2636.

[29]   Klein, G. (2007). Performing a Project Premortem. Harvard Business Review. 85 (9): 18-19. (https://hbr.org/2007/09/performing-a-project-premortem)

[30]   Brown, P. (2007). Analyzing Failure Beforehand. New York Times. (Available at: https://www.nytimes.com/2007/09/22/business/media/22offline.html)

[31] Shull, F., Basili, V. R. et al. (2002). What We Have Learned About Fighting Defects. Proc. 8th International Software Metrics Symposium, 2002, pp. 39-42.

[32] Reinertsen, D. G. (2012). The Principles of Product Development Flow: Second Generation Lean Product Development. Celeritas Publishing.

[33] Red Team. Wikipedia. https://en.wikipedia.org/wiki/Red_team.

[34] Scaled Agile Framework®. https://www.scaledagileframework.com. (Version 5.0 of the framework.)

[35] Large-Scale Scrum (LeSS). https://less.works.

[36] Larman, C. & Vodde, B. (2010). Practices for Scaling Lean & Agile Development: Large, Multisite, and Offshore Product Development with Large-Scale Scrum. Addison-Wesley Professional.

[37] Skelton, M. & Pais, M. (2019). Team Topologies: Organizing Business and Technology Teams for Fast Flow. IT Revolution Press.

[38] Schwartz, M. (2016). The Art of Business Value. IT Revolution Press.

[39] Leffingwell, D. (2010). Agile Software Requirements: Lean Requirements Practices for Teams, Programs, and the Enterprise. Addison-Wesley Professional.

[40] Linear Programming. Wikipedia. https://en.wikipedia.org/wiki/Linear_programming.

[41] The Sveriges Riksbank Prize in Economic Sciences in Memory of Alfred Nobel 1975. The Nobel Prize. https://www.nobelprize.org/prizes/economic-sciences/1975/summary/.

[42] Vector Space. Wikipedia. https://en.wikipedia.org/wiki/Vector_space.

[43] Graphical Linear Programming for Two Variables. Wolfram Demonstration Project. https://demonstrations.wolfram.com/GraphicalLinearProgrammingForTwoVariables/.

[44] Nonlinear Programming. MIT. https://web.mit.edu/15.053/www/AMP-Chapter-13.pdf.

[45] Riesz Space. Encyclopedia of Mathematics. https://encyclope-diaofmath.org/wiki/Riesz_space.

[46] Schaefer, H. H. (2011). Banach Lattices and Positive Operators. Springer Berlin Heidelberg.

[47] Lexicographical Order. Wikipedia. https://en.wikipedia.org/wiki/Lexicographical_order.

[48] Function Space. Wikipedia. https://en.wikipedia.org/wiki/Function_space.

[49] The Vector Space of Polynomials in x With Rational Coefficients. School of Mathematics and Statistics. https://people.math.carleton. ca/~kcheung/math/notes/MATH1107/wk08/08_infinite_dimen- sion_example.html.

[50] Dot Product. Paul's Notes. https://tutorial.math.lamar.edu/classes/ calcii/dotproduct.aspx.

[51] Power Law. Wikipedia. https://en.wikipedia.org/wiki/Power_law.

[52] Pareto Principle. Wikipedia. https://en.wikipedia.org/wiki/ Pareto_principle.

[53] Louridas, P., Spinellis, D. & Vlachos, V. (2008). Power Laws in Software. TOSEM'08, vol. 18, no. 1, Sep 2008.

[54] WordNet, Degree Distribution. Konect. http://konect.uni-koblenz. de/networks/wordnet-words.

[55] Nie, L. et al. Bridging the Vocabulary Gap between Health Seekers and Healthcare Knowledge. (2015). IEEE Transactions on Knowledge and Data Engineering (TKDE). 27, (2), 1041-4347. Research Collection School Of Information Systems. (Available at: https://ink.library.smu.edu.sg/sis_research/2252)

[56] Reeve L. H. et al. (2006). Concept frequency distribution in bio- medical text summarization. In: 15th ACM international conference on information and knowledge management; 2006. p. 604–11. (Available at: https://dl.acm.org/doi/pdf/10.1145/1183614.1183701)

[57] Stack Exchange. https://stackexchange.com/sites.

[58] Evolution. Wikipedia. https://en.wikipedia.org/wiki/Evolution.

[59] Disruptive Selection. Biology Dictionary. https://biologydictionary. net/disruptive-selection/.

[60] Stabilizing Selection. Biology Dictionary. https://biologydictionary. net/stabilizing-selection/.

[61] Horizontal Gene Transfer. Encyclopædia Britannica. https://www. britannica.com/science/horizontal-gene-transfer.

[62] Phylogenetic Tree. Wikipedia. https://en.wikipedia.org/wiki/ Phylogenetic_tree.

[63] Convergent Evolution. Live Science. https://www.livescience.com/ convergent-evolution.html/.

[64] Nonaka I. & Takeuchi, H. (1995). The Knowledge-creating Company: How Japanese Companies Create the Dynamics of Innovation. Oxford University Press.

[65] SECI Model of Knowledge Dimensions. Wikipedia. https://en.wiki- pedia.org/wiki/SECI_model_of_knowledge_dimensions.

[66] PDCA. Wikipedia. https://en.wikipedia.org/wiki/PDCA.

[67] OODA Loop. Wikipedia. https://en.wikipedia.org/wiki/OODA_loop.

[68] Wolfgram, C. G., & Goldstein, M. L. (1987). The search for the physical basis of memory. Bulletin of the Psychonomic Society, 25, 65–68. (Available at: https://link.springer.com/content/pdf/10.3758/BF03330080.pdf)

[69] Snowden, D. J. (2016). A Return to Constraints. Cognitive Edge. https://www.cognitive-edge.com/blog/a-return-to-constraints/.

[70] Poppendieck, M. (2003). Lean Development and the Predictability Paradox. Cutter Consortium. http://www.poppendieck.com/pdfs/Predictability_Paradox.pdf.

[71] Wake, B. Small – Scalable – Stories in the INVEST Model. https://xp123.com/articles/small-scalable-stories-in-the-invest-model/.

[72] Wake, B. Twenty Ways to Split Stories. https://xp123.com/articles/twenty-ways-to-split-stories/.

[73] Dynamical System. Wikipedia. https://en.wikipedia.org/wiki/Dynamical_system.

[74] Nobel laureate Daniel Kahneman – Premortem to eliminate thinking biases. YouTube. https://www.youtube.com/watch?v=MzTNMalfyhM.

[75] Bacteria Cell Structure. https://micro.magnet.fsu.edu/cells/bacteriacell.html.

[76] Tagkopoulos, I., Liu, Y., & Tavazoie, S. (2008). Predictive behavior within microbial genetic networks. Science, 320 5881, 1313-7 .

[77] Scientists Teach Worms to Learn. Phys.Org. https://phys.org/news/2005-11-scientists-worms.html.

[78] Strongest Evidence of Animal Culture Seen in Monkeys and Whales. Science. https://www.sciencemag.org/news/2013/04/strongest-evidence-animal-culture-seen-monkeys-and-whales.

[79] Does Losing One Sense Improve the Others. Science ABC. https://www.scienceabc.com/humans/does-losing-one-sense-improve-the-others.html.

[80] Exaptation. Wikipedia. https://en.wikipedia.org/wiki/Exaptation.

[81] Resource Curse. Wikipedia. https://en.wikipedia.org/wiki/Resource_curse https://en.wikipedia.org/wiki/Resource_curse

[82] Incidence Matrix. Wikipedia. https://en.wikipedia.org/wiki/Incidence_matrix.

[83] Adzic, G. (2011). Specification by Example: How Successful Teams Deliver the Right Software. Manning Publications.

[84] Humble, J. & Farley, D. (2010). Continuous Delivery: Reliable Software Releases through Build, Test, and Deployment Automation. Addison-Wesley Professional.

[85] Kim, Gene et al. (2016). The DevOps Handbook: How to Create World-Class Agility, Reliability, and Security in Technology Organizations. IT Revolution Press.

[86] Driska, A. (2019). Good coaching is the effective manipulation of task constraints, not just telling athletes how to perform. Michigan State University. https://education.msu.edu/sport-coaching-leadership/food4thought/teaching-and-refining-athletic-skill/.

[87] Altitude training. Wikipedia. https://en.wikipedia.org/wiki/Altitude_training.

[88] Edmondson, A. C. (2011). Strategies for learning from failure, Harvard Business Review, April 2011. (Available at: https://hbr.org/2011/04/strategies-for-learning-from-failure)

[89] Project re:Work. With Google. https://rework.withgoogle.com/print/guides/5721312655835136/.

[90] Twelve Leverage Points. Wikipedia. *https://en.wikipedia.org/wiki/Twelve_leverage_points*.

Index

T

task lifecycle tracking 20
technical debt 55, 69, 70, 72, 107
test automation 180, 182, 183, 193, 198, 223, 235, 239
test-first 110
the chasm 67, 68, 229
trust 149, 186, 187, 191, 197, 198, 205, 212, 220, 223, 228, 229, 233, 247, 248

U

ultimate outcome 47, 62, 64, 65, 103, 124, 171, 218
ultimate value 171
unknowns 27, 78, 79, 81, 82, 92, 93, 94, 95, 96, 97, 98, 99, 100, 101, 103, 104, 105, 108, 109, 111, 115, 118, 135, 136, 138, 149, 165, 168, 173, 213, 214, 248, 268
usability 20, 57, 70, 226
usage context 22

usage data 35
user scenarios 146, 251
utility 120, 171, 212, 225, 249, 254, 264, 271, 272, 279

V

value-action gap 27, 266
value discovery 123, 128, 133, 138, 141, 149, 156, 159, 168, 171, 173, 174, 176, 177, 269
value moderator 138, 139, 140, 156
value path 122, 125, 126, 127, 128, 132, 135, 136, 137, 138, 139, 140, 141, 144, 145, 146, 148, 149, 155, 159, 160, 161, 164, 175, 177, 254
value path map 125, 137
value score 123, 128, 141, 175, 177
versatile asset 150, 153, 154, 156
vertical slice 222, 223

Z

zero-day 74

Made in the USA
Monee, IL
03 September 2020